# (MUCH) MORE FROM
# OVER THE RAINBOW BRIDGE

First Impression – 2006

ISBN 0-9548019-1-1

© Wendy M. Tugby

Published by Wendy M. Tugby

British Library Cataloguing-in-Publication Data
A catalogue record for this book is available from the British Library.

*Printed in Wales at*
*Gomer Press, Llandysul, Ceredigion SA44 4JL*

# (Much) More From Over the Rainbow Bridge

Wendy M. Tugby

*To*
*Sweep –*

*because but for him, we might still not understand*

*and*

**to all our beloved animals  -**

*for the love and devotion of those remaining with us in this life and for the continued and most welcome presence of those that have preceded us to the next*

# Acknowledgements

Firstly, my thanks to all those who have my first book, 'Over The Rainbow Bridge', for your letters, telephone calls and e-mails of encouragement and support for this, the follow-up.

Next, my grateful and heartfelt thanks to all who have contributed stories for this second book and once again thankyou, not only for entrusting me with your most private and personal experiences but also, for giving your permission for them to be published; ultimately I hope, for the benefit of those who find themselves in similar situations.

Many of you, the majority in fact, have given permission for your real names to be used in this book. I believe that this is real progress – and such a difference from two years ago when the first Rainbow Bridge book was published.

When I embarked on that book, virtually every one who contributed asked that their name be changed for publication, just in case other people might think they were strange – or unhinged, if their real identity were known.

The subject of After Death Communication, even that short space of time ago, was very much taboo and few would openly admit to even an interest in it, let alone profess to have experienced it. Now, it's very much an 'in' subject – everyone's talking about it and why not?

It's amazing how many people, in the course of the most normal of conversations, will relate a tale of a 'visit' from a departed friend - and have you noticed how many television programmes there are now, that deal with the subject of the afterlife?

It seems that there could well be hundreds, (possibly thousands), of we 'strange' people about after all and – by the time you reach the end of this book, you'll see that we're in very good company!

\*\*\*\*\*

On a personal note; to those readers of 'Over The Rainbow Bridge' who have written thanking me for the comfort, hope and reassurance it's given them, I would like to say how deeply moved and humbled I have been by your letters and e-mails. Thank you all - I hope this second book brings comfort, hope and reassurance to many more.

*****

My thanks are also due to the following publishers, for their kind permission to use extracts from the books mentioned.

Extract from '*Angela's Ashes*' by Frank McCourt.
Reprinted by permission of HarperCollins Publishers Ltd.
© Frank McCourt. (First published in 1996)

Extract from '*Wild Stone Heart*' by Sharon Butala.
Published by VIrago Press. 2001
Reprinted by permission of Little, Brown Book Group.

Extracts from '*Many Mansions*'(1943) and '*Lychgate*'(1945),
by Lord Dowding,
Published by Rider & Co.Ltd (Random House Group Ltd.)
Reprinted by permission of David Higham Associates Ltd.

*The Power Of The Dog*', by Rudyard Kipling.
Featured in 'Faithful to the end; "Daily Telegraph" Anthology of Dogs' by Celia Haddon.
Published by Headline Book Publishing Ltd. (1991)
Reprinted by permission of A.P. Watt Ltd., on behalf of the National Trust for PLaces of Historic Interest or Natural Beauty.

# Contents

**To Native American (Shaman) Indians, the Rainbow Bridge
is known as the way into the spirit world.**

# The Rainbow Bridge

'Just this side of Heaven is a place called the Rainbow Bridge. When a hound dies that has been especially close to someone here, that dog goes to Rainbow Bridge. There are meadows and hills for all our special friends so they run and play together. There is plenty of food and water and sunshine and our friends are warm and comfortable. All the hounds that are old or ill are restored to health and vigour. Those who were hurt or maimed are made whole and strong again, just as we remember them in our dreams of days and times gone by.

The hounds are happy and content except for one small thing – they each miss someone special to them who had to be left behind. They all run and play together but the day comes when one suddenly stops and looks into the distance. The bright eyes are intent, the eager body quivers. Suddenly he begins to run from the group, flying over the green grass, his legs carrying him faster and faster. YOU have been spotted and when you and your special friend finally meet, you cling together in joyous reunion, never to be parted again. The happy kisses rain upon your face, your hands again caress the beloved head and you look once more into the trusting eyes of your hound so long gone from your life but never absent from your heart. Then you cross the Rainbow Bridge together.'

Anon.

*****

According to the Bible, the Rainbow is a sign from God -

**I do set my bow in the cloud, and it shall be for a token of a
covenant between me and the earth.**

**The original version of the Rainbow Bridge relates specifically to dogs, so, for those of you who have other kinds of pets, here is the alternative version -**

# *The Rainbow Bridge*

'Just this side of Heaven is a place called Rainbow Bridge. When an animal dies that has been especially close to someone here, that pet goes to Rainbow Bridge.

There are meadows and hills for all of our special friends so they can run and play together. There is plenty of food and water and sunshine, and our friends are warm and comfortable. All the animals who have been ill and old are restored to health and vigour: those who were hurt or maimed are made whole and strong again, just as we remember them in our dreams of days and times gone by.

The animals are happy and content, except for one small thing; they miss someone very special to them, who had to be left behind. They run and play together, but the day comes when one suddenly stops and looks into the distance. The bright eyes are intent; the eager body quivers. Suddenly he begins to break away from the group, flying over the green grass, his legs carrying him faster and faster. YOU have been spotted and when you and your special friend finally meet, you cling together in joyous reunion, never to be parted again. The happy kisses rain upon your face, your hands again caress the beloved head and you look once more into the trusting eyes of your pet, so long gone from your life but never absent from your heart. Then you cross the Rainbow Bridge, together.'

Anon.

*****

# A poem for the grieving

Do not stand at my grave and weep.
I am not there, I do not sleep.
I am a thousand winds that blow,
I am the diamond glints on snow.
I am the sunlight on ripened grain,
I am the gentle autumn's rain.
When you awaken in the morning's hush,
I am the swift uplifting rush
Of quiet birds in circled flight.
I am the soft stars that shine at night.
Do not stand at my grave and cry;
I am not there. I did not die.

Author Unknown

# Contact From The Other Side

Those of you who have read *'Over The Rainbow Bridge'*, (OTRB), will now be familiar with the ways in which our animals, (and loved ones), can and do, make contact with us, after they have left this earthly life. For the benefit of those who have not read 'OTRB' and who are perhaps still unaware of the many possible means of contact, an explanation follows.

Thanks are due once more to Bill and Judy Guggenheim, co-authors of *'Hello From Heaven'*, a book which contains more than three hundred and fifty accounts of human After Death Communication (referred to as ADC's), selected from over 3,300 firsthand accounts, collected over a period of approximately seven years.

That we have as much information to hand on the subject as we do, is largely thanks to their painstaking and pioneering research.

In *'Hello From Heaven'*, the authors identify several main ways in which those that have passed make contact with us, the most common of these being: - sense (Sentient), sound (Auditory), smell (Olfactory), sight (Visual), touch (Tactile), dreams (Dream-State) and visions. The use of symbols (Symbolic) and physical phenomena is also quite common and each ADC may contain just one or two of these elements, or a combination of several.

Again, from the accounts of animal ADC's that have been sent to me, there would appear to be little difference between the ways in which our departed pets and our departed loved ones, make contact with us.

If nothing else, the process of writing/compiling *'Over The Rainbow Bridge'* and this, the follow-up book, has taught me to keep an open mind and rule nothing out. It seems, that when those that have crossed over want to get in touch, anything can - and does, happen!

A brief explanation of each of the more general types of contact follows but there may well be others, not included here, that are equally valid for those who experience them.

# Methods of Contact Explained

**Sense, (Sentient).** This is when the 'presence' of the departed loved one is felt. Each visit has a beginning and an end and experiencers have the distinct feeling that their loved one is with them, even though they may not be able to see them.

**Sound (Auditory).** Hearing a voice, or familiar noise. This can either be heard in the normal way, i.e. externally, through the ears; or internally, i.e. inside the head or the mind but originating from an outside source, as with telepathy.

**Smell (Olfactory).** When the presence of a smell, fragrance, aroma, is noticed, which belongs unmistakeably to the one who has passed.

**Sight (Visual).** When the deceased loved one makes either a full or partial appearance.

With a partial appearance they may be - (a) only partly visible, (b) wholly visible but not solid, or, (c) they may appear in, or as, a brilliant light.

With a full appearance, the whole body is seen, solid - as in this life and always healed of any former illness or disability. In particular, these appearances generally give their experiencers great comfort and/or healing.

**Dreams (Sleep-state).** Easily distinguishable from ordinary dreams, because they are more vivid, colourful and real. Also, details of events stay clearly in the minds of experiencers, even years afterwards.

This is a very common kind of ADC, probably because the mind is more relaxed and open when asleep.

Similarly, contact of any kind may occur when you are just dozing, daydreaming, or on the point of sleeping or waking up. Again, the mind is relaxed and receptive.

**Symbols (Symbolic).** Butterflies (a symbol for the Resurrection) and moths. Rainbows, feathers and flowers are all spirit signs. Birds, animals and even everyday objects can also be signs.

Interpretation is up to the individual but when a sign appears, there is no mistaking that it is indeed a sign, though John Edward, (a spiritual medium, now well-known through his television programme 'Crossing Over', on Living TV – satellite channel), advises that we should not look too hard for signs in case we miss the subtle sign that is the true message.

**Physical Phenomena.**  These include windows and doors opening or closing; objects moving; lights and all kinds of electrical devices being switched on or off; pictures moving and clocks and watches stopping.

There are other less common methods of contact.  These include -

**Touch (Tactile).**    The experiencer feels actual physical contact in some way, from the departed loved one.

**Visions**.  These may be, (a) external, i.e. outwardly seen with the eyes, or, (b) internal, i.e. in the mind.

   In either case they appear as brightly coloured films or slides, either floating in the air, or, as though the experiencer was looking through a screen.

**ADCs that happen before the experiencer is aware of death occurring.**  Proof that ADC's are not imagination, hallucinations, or grief-induced memories.

**Shared ADCs.**    When more than one person experiences contact simultaneously.

**Evidential.**  When something is made known to you that you neither knew, nor had any way of knowing, beforehand; e.g. where something has been hidden.

**Out of Body ADCs.**  When the earthly being leaves their earthly body, (usually feeling they are rising above it, so that they can see it below them), in order to meet with the spirit of their departed loved one.

   *In 'Over The Rainbow Bridge', the story of Lace's 'visit' to Sue, the faith healer who was treating her for Lymphosarcoma, would suggest that there are other possibilities  and the story of Amanda and Tia in this book, provides yet another slant on the same phenomenon.*

**ADCs for the prevention of suicide.** The intervention of the departed loved one, to stop their loved one on this side taking his or her own life.

*I have to admit that I didn't think I would hear an account of this last one in connection with an animal ADC and in fact, I omitted it from 'Over The Rainbow Bridge' for that reason – but I was wrong – so much for an open mind! The first e-mail that I received from a reader of 'OTRB', was from Cynthia, who was replying to my request for stories for this follow-up book. Her account is testimony to the fact that our departed animals can intervene for our safety.*

*See 'Cynthia and Cimmie' p.48.*

Hope is the thing with feathers
that perches in the soul
And sings the tune without the words
and never stops – at all.


Emily Dickinson

(1830 – 86)

# 'Over the Rainbow Bridge'

As readers of 'OTRB' will know, our own story began in February 2003, with the loss of Sweep, a twenty-two month old Irish Wolfhound, following which, we experienced many strange happenings and 'visits' from Sweep himself. Fortunately, from the time they began, I had noted these events in a diary and they were the catalyst for the book.

In May 2004, we had to have Molly (Irish Wolfhound) put to sleep, at almost ten years of age. She was Sweep's friend and mentor and taught him his manners.

2005 was not a good year for us. In February we lost Sweep's sister, Mole, (three years, ten months). In May we lost his uncle, Bozo, (seven and a half years). Then, in June, we lost his niece, Chelsea, (seventeen months) and finally, in October, we lost his mum, Slinky, (seven years, eleven months).

Every loss hit us hard - none were expected and we mourn the loss of all those who have left us; though we appreciate that they don't come with any guarantee of how long they are going to stay.

Each dog we lost had to be put to sleep to end his, or her, suffering but without exception, each has made contact since leaving, either by sending a sign, which thankfully we now recognise as such, or, by putting in an appearance. It warms our hearts to know they are still very much around. That doesn't stop us missing* them of course but it helps the healing process.

Now, we treasure every day with our present ones and we're so grateful to have the privilege of their company.

They say that true love means setting those you love free. We hope we've been able to do that for each of our animals, when the time has been right.

*****

\*On the subject of 'missing' our departed loved ones, I was watching television yesterday, 13th. July '06, around 6pm, which is something I rarely do at that time but I was killing time waiting for the dinner to finish cooking. Flipping through the channels, I came to 'Crossing Over' with John Edward. I hadn't seen the programme for ages, so I just had to watch it. Right at the end, John said something, which, to me, makes perfect sense. He said, that he didn't believe our departed loved ones miss us, because they know they are still with us and so still 'have' us but, they validate their presence to us, (in the form of ADC's), to reassure us that they are still very much around and part of our lives - because we miss them………

\*\*\*\*\*

# Visits From Our Own Dogs

As in 'Over The Rainbow Bridge', I'll start if I may,
with the stories of those of our own dogs mentioned
previously and the ways in which they've let us know
they are still with us and keeping an eye on our comings
and goings.

*****

# *Molly*

May 2004. We had been over to Southern Ireland with the dogs, to do what is known as the 'Mini Circuit'. This consists of three different shows, on three consecutive days.

At the second show, on the Sunday, Steve had won through to the group with Bailey, (the young dog we fetched from Ireland after we lost Sweep – 'OTRB'), and as they were in the group ring, a Red Admiral flew right in front of his face. It must have brought him luck because he was Reserve overall, to an outstanding Whippet that went on to win Best In Show.

Earlier in the week he'd seen a Red Admiral in the garden and he'd also had one in his lorry when he left the window down. Sweep obviously knew we were off to Ireland!

We were due to return home on Tuesday May 4th. On the Monday evening, I rang our dog-sitter, to ask if everything was OK at home and all the dogs well. She said that she thought Molly had come in season, as she'd noticed blood on her bed and that the bed was also quite wet where she'd been trying to clean herself. Alarm bells rang immediately because I knew Molly had been in season at the beginning of March and I straight away suspected an open Pyometra. The dog sitter said she seemed alright in herself and was still eating and drinking normally, so I just asked that she keep an eye on her and call the vet immediately if she was worried about her.

We arrived home the next day, Tuesday, in the afternoon and Molly was at the gate to greet us, tail wagging as always but quite obviously not her normal self. When the dog-sitter had left, I phoned our vet and explained the situation to him. He knew Molly well and was aware that she had been getting increasingly frail with age and very wobbly on her hind legs. He said she undoubtedly had an open Pyometra and that, in view of her age, antibiotics were unlikely to work successfully and the only alternative was a total hysterectomy. As far as I was concerned, that was not an option. At her age, I was not prepared to let her face major surgery and the possibility (and real danger - particularly for Wolfhounds), of dying under anaesthetic.

We had two more days of her company and spoilt her in every way we could think of.  She was put to sleep on her bed in the dog room on the morning of Friday 7th. May.

She went easily and peacefully.  The vet did say that it was absolutely the right decision, as she would not have survived the anaesthetic had she been operated on.  Steve took her body to the vet's later that day, to be cremated.

The other dogs were very quiet after she'd gone.  She was our oldest and longest-lived Wolfhound and seemed to have been about forever.  She had brought up all of our puppies; teaching them manners and proper Wolfhound conduct; though sadly, she'd never had puppies of her own.  The house seemed so empty without her.

On the morning of Sunday 9th May, Steve had been outside pressure-washing the lorry and stopped for a call of nature.  He walked indoors, through the kitchen, through the dog-room and into the downstairs toilet.  Passing Molly on her bed as he walked through the dog-room, he said 'Hya Molls,' as normal and went into the toilet, closing the door behind him.  As soon as he'd closed the door he realised what had just happened.  He very quietly and carefully opened the door and peeped round it to see if she was still there but she'd gone.

I can't tell you how I felt when he told me.  I didn't know whether to laugh or cry, or jump for joy and I probably did all three; I was so happy to know that she was still about.

*Unlike Steve, I've never yet been lucky enough to 'see' one of our hounds after they've passed but I have had two 'visits', (plus another since), that I know were Molly. -*

The first was within a week of her being put to sleep.  I was standing at the sink in the kitchen, preparing vegetables for dinner, when I felt a nudge on my bottom at about the height of a Wolfhound nose.  I turned round immediately to see who it was but the kitchen was empty – none of the hounds were indoors.  I thought I must have imagined it.  Two days later, I was standing by the work surface at the back of the kitchen when I felt a nudge on my bottom again and very distinct this time.  I spun round but again – no dogs about.  I laughed then and said 'Hello Molly' because I just knew it was her.

Before I knew about the ways in which we can be contacted, I would have missed this sign completely and probably just put it down to the involuntary twitching of a muscle but this was an external sensation, not an internal one; a really soft nudge on each occasion but unmistakable and after the second time it happened, I knew it was Molly because that had always been her way of attracting your attention - by poking you, though usually in the shins with her front paw.  Then she would grin at you with her lips drawn back so it was impossible not to laugh at her.

It is so comforting to know she is still around.

*(see photo page 71)*

# Sweep

*Sunday 25th. July 2004.*

Steve had a 'visit' from Sweep, in his usual manner, i.e. in a sleep-state dream. ('OTRB')

As always, I had woken from my sleep, or rather, been woken, by Steve's mutterings. I immediately realised what was happening, even though it had been a while since Sweep's last visit. I kept very still and quiet until I knew it was over.

When Steve woke, I said ' Your pal's been then?'

'Yes', he said 'but I had to visit him this time.'

With all the previous visits, Sweep has always come to Steve but this time, as Steve explained, he felt compelled to go to visit Sweep instead.

He said that, at first, when he started out on his visit to Sweep, he was travelling very slowly but then he speeded up and it was as though he was passing points of light (I wondered if they were stars perhaps?), until eventually, Sweep was there playing round his feet. Everything was green and in a mist. Sweep looked very happy and well. He played a lot and was bounding about but on his own. Eventually, he looked into the distance and trotted off, came back and then trotted off again and faded.

*Strangely enough; (or maybe not); while I was in the barn yesterday, (Saturday 24th July '04), writing out one of the stories for the new book, a Red Admiral had appeared and fluttered about while I was working. Later on, when I told Steve, he'd remarked that Sweep didn't come to see him any more, then that very night he had his sleep-state dream where he went to visit Sweep.*

*Puts me in mind of what my mother used to say – 'Well you can always come and see me you know.'*

*(see photo page 67)*

# Chelsea & Alfie's Strange Behaviour

*September 2004*

*C**helsea and Alfie are Sweep's niece and nephew, born December 30th. 2003. Their mum Zizi, is his (and Mole's) sister. They were eight months old when the following happened.*

Steve and I were sitting in the lounge one evening. The TV was on. Chelsea was lying on the floor in front of the settee and Alfie was lying on the settee. Both were fast asleep. Suddenly, Chelsea jumped up and started to woof (in single woofs, with a space between each one), in the direction of one of the stereo speakers, which stands on a little shelf, quite high up on the wall, next to the full height pine cupboard just inside the lounge door and behind the settee where she had been lying.

She never once took her eyes off the speaker.

We both watched her in amazement and I asked Steve if the sound from the TV came out through the speaker (I'm not very technically minded but I didn't think it did) and he confirmed that, no, it didn't. Next thing, Alfie leapt off the settee and started sniffing the carpet in front of Steve's chair on the opposite side of the room.

We couldn't help wondering just who was about.

# Monday October 4th. 2004.
# Orbs In The Barn

Steve had finished work early and we took a cup of tea through to the lounge. As we opened the lounge door, we heard fluttering and there in the window facing onto the patio, were two Red Admiral butterflies.

We wondered how they'd got in, as the door and the windows in the lounge had all been closed and eventually we decided that they must have come in by the bedroom window and flown downstairs.

We sat down with our tea and watched them fluttering away in the window until one flew across the room into the window next to where Steve was sitting. A minute or so later, the other one did the same thing. I told Steve he better let them out, before they damaged their wings. He opened the window but they resisted all his attempts to evict them, so he gave up, closed the window and left them where they were. We finished our tea and both went off to do different jobs. Later, when we returned to the lounge, they'd gone.

Around 6.30pm that evening, Steve went through to the barn to fiddle about on the computer as he usually does. I was upstairs when he called me to come down and see what he'd done.

'I've just photographed an orb,'* he said.

He'd seen an orb out of the corner of his eye, (very unusual) and picked up the digital camera, which is always by the side of the computer, switched it on, swung round in the chair and clicked, in the hope that he might catch something. He downloaded it onto the computer and what he'd managed to capture, was not just one but two orbs, which we thought was really exciting - especially after seeing the butterflies earlier.

Steve asked 'What's the date today?'

*(This tends to be an automatic response with us now, whenever anything slightly out of the ordinary happens.)*

I looked at the calendar and said 'The fourth of October.'

'I wonder what the significance of that is then?' he said but neither of us had any idea.

We tried to recall if we'd lost any dogs, or had any put to sleep, or even had any born on that date, but nothing rang a bell. In the end we couldn't think of any connection at all, so we just put it down to a casual visit.

How silly of us!

*****

*An orb is a floating circle or point of light, thought to represent the presence of spirit, frequently caught on camera but rarely seen with the naked eye.*

*(See photo page 72)*

# Angela's Ashes

Lately, I've been trying to work my way through all the books on my bookshelves that I haven't yet read. Round about the middle of last week, (October 6th/7th '04), I started one that I've had for several years but for some reason, have always pushed aside before.

The book in question, a true story, is 'Angela's Ashes', by Frank McCourt. I came across this extract on Tuesday 12th. October, 2004.

\*\*\*\*\*

'There's a picture on another wall of a man with a brown robe and birds sitting all over him. Fintan says, Do you know who that is, Francis? No? That's your patron, St. Francis of Assisi,* and do you know what today is?

*The fourth of October.*

That's right and it's his feast day and special for you because you can ask St. Francis for anything and he'll surely give it to you.'

\*\*\*\*\*

*So, now we know the significance of the fourth of October.*

*St. Francis is, of course, the patron saint of animals.

# *Mole*

*February 2005.*

Sweep's sister, Mole, had injured her back in September last year and though we made her rest as much as possible, it was extremely difficult to keep a live wire like her quiet. We took her for chiropractic sessions, which seemed to improve things at first and gave us hope that she might recover but her condition deteriorated, until she was in too much pain to have an acceptable quality of life.

An operation was discussed with our vet and ruled out, so, although she was only three years and ten months old, the decision was made to euthanase her, to prevent further suffering. She was put to sleep at home on Wednesday, 23rd. February.

Later that same day, Steve took her body to the vet's to be cremated. He had arranged to take her in after surgery finished, around 7p.m. but he left home a little early and decided to stop at the beach with her, to watch the sunset. He was talking to her and said it was time for her to go to play with Sweep now. Then he turned on the van radio and what should be playing but 'Spirit In The Sky'* and he knew that Sweep had come to fetch his sister.

*****

---

* 'OTRB'. Page 28. How 'Spirit In The Sky' became Sweep's alternative name. His real (KC registered) name was …'Smoke On The Water'……..

# Bozo

Sweep's uncle, Bozo, was put to sleep. He was taken ill yesterday, very suddenly. As far as we were aware, he had been perfectly healthy up to that point, still bouncing about, eating well and howling like mad to greet us each time we returned from an outing.

We had noticed of late that he was getting a little weak behind but we put that down to his age. He was a large framed dog and seven and a half years old and we thought it was just a natural progression. The only other problem he'd had, several weeks prior to his death, was that he'd made the end of his tail bleed by banging it against the wire of his run and I had to resort to putting a foam tube cover on it, to protect it from continual damage. It did heal eventually but it took much longer than I would have expected.

On Tuesday 24th, he ate his breakfast readily, jumping up as always, with his front feet on top of the hurdles dividing the drive, in his impatience to be fed. He had a tiny choke after his feed, just clearing his throat once, as though a morsel of food had gone down the wrong way. I said 'Poor boy', in mock sympathy and then he seemed fine.

Steve had a dental appointment that afternoon, at 3pm. I put the dogs away at 2.15pm, just before we left. Bozo trotted into his run, along with Slinky, his sister and Rio (Steve's one remaining Great Dane) and again, all seemed fine.

We arrived home at 5pm and weren't met with the usual howling, which I immediately thought was odd. I went straight away to open their run, as I always did first thing we returned home and Slinky came out from the kennel into the run but no Bozo. I called him and he came out very slowly, head down, definitely not himself. I noticed two patches of white, frothy, watery sick in the run. I quickly checked the return on his gums and felt his belly, fearing the dreaded bloat/torsion. He was breathing heavily and fast and although he wasn't bloated, everything else pointed to a torsion of some kind.

I called to Steve, who had parked the van up by then and told him there was something seriously the matter with Bozo.  He came to look and suggested it might be a heart attack, which seemed equally possible.

I asked him to phone the vet straight away.  He ran into the house and then ran out again – no phone!  We'd both forgotten that it had been out of order since the previous Thursday night and BT weren't due to fix it until Wednesday 25th, - the next day.

Living up in the mountains, we can't usually get a signal on the mobiles but by standing on the front road fence, Steve got enough of a signal to phone the vet, who said to get Bozo straight to the surgery.  He (the vet) was out on call but said he would get there as soon as possible.

When we arrived at the surgery, only the duty vet was there, though she had been warned to expect us.  She took Bozo's temperature, which was 105, checked his heart and lungs and said he had a throat infection, which I queried, as he seemed much too ill for it to be merely a throat infection but she put him on a drip and gave him an antibiotic and anti-inflammatory straight into the vein, took a blood sample for analysis and said she wanted us to ring the next morning and if he was OK, to take him back the same time next day for further antibiotics etc.

Back home, we spread a big quilt on the floor of the lounge and Bozo spent the evening with us.  The only reason he didn't usually do this, was because Bailey and Alfie, (father and son), both live indoors and unfortunately, they didn't get on with Bozo, nor he with them.

He spent a peaceful night.  Steve took his temperature before he left for work the next morning.  It was down to 102.1 but there was no improvement in his overall condition and after standing for ten minutes, the muscles in his back legs went into spasm and I had to persuade him to lie down again.   I asked Steve to phone the vet while he was out, for the results of the blood tests.

During the morning, Bozo had an occasional drink of water but apart from a tiny amount of tinned food, would not eat.  I gave him a brush, in preparation for, what I already knew in my heart, was going to be his last journey and told him repeatedly how much I loved him.  I said it was time for him to be with Jenna (his mum) and Molly and

Mole and asked if he would say hello to them for me and tell them I love them too and I asked if he would come and see me some time and let me know he'd arrived safely and was OK and happy. I sat with him in the lounge, reading and watching him lying peacefully on his quilt and although he was breathing hard, he didn't seem in pain.

Steve arrived home later that morning but in a van instead of the lorry. When I asked where the lorry was, he said a car had hit him head-on, just outside the village. The lorry was at the garage where he has his maintenance work done and they'd lent him the van to get home with. 'But' he said 'That's not the bad news.' I knew straight away what he meant.

I said 'It's Bozo, isn't it?'

'Yes', he said, - 'he has leukaemia.'

And all I could say was, 'I'm not surprised. I knew it was going to be bad.'

The vet had run the blood test twice and found no white cell count at all. Steve had asked about a blood transfusion but was told it would not be of any use, that the only thing for leukaemia is a bone marrow transplant and as yet, they only do that with humans and not dogs. The vet had said for us to take Bozo to the surgery that evening, to discuss where we went from there but I felt that he had been through enough and took the decision to have him put to sleep, at home.

So, Steve went out a little while later and phoned the vet. Bozo was put to sleep peacefully, at 2.30pm that afternoon, on his quilt in the lounge. We took his body to the surgery for cremation later that evening.


*Thursday 26th. May*


At last, BT had fixed the phone. At 8pm on the 26th, I rang my son Daniel, (who lives in Norfolk), for the first time in a week and told him about Bozo.

I was still on the phone to him at 9pm., when suddenly, there was a large brown moth flying round the lounge. Although the lounge light was on, it was still daylight outside. I was really surprised and said to Daniel, 'Oh, a great big moth has just flown in', and I was giving him a running commentary on its strange behaviour, though neither of us could quite believe what was happening and all Steve, (who hates moths), could say, was 'Kill it', while I was frantically trying to stop him swatting it and telling him to leave it alone; until even he realised there was something very unusual going on.

After flying round the lounge a couple of times, the moth flew to the two large Wolfhound prints on the wall behind the chair where I was sitting. It landed on one of the two hounds on the print, then moved directly to the other one, hovering for a while on each one; then moved to the next print and did exactly the same with the two hounds on that one. It then moved up the wall to the image of the Great Dane on the clock-face. From there it flew straight to Sweep's photograph and hovered on Sweep; moved across to Steve (still on the photograph) and then settled on the bottom left-hand corner of the photo frame, folded its' wings and remained there, unmoving, until we went to bed at 11pm. The next morning it was gone.

### Friday 27th. May

It was a very hot day. We had been out and arrived back at around 5.30pm. I let the dogs out and then went into the lounge. It felt hot and stuffy in there, so I went to open the window. This has a top section, which is hinged at the top and swings open when you release the two catches in the middle, which secure it to the bottom section. I pushed the window open and as I looked back to where I'd just seconds before released the catches, there was the moth, resting wings folded, exactly where the right-hand catch on the window had been. I knew it couldn't possibly have been there before, as the catch would have caught it on the way up. It stayed perfectly still while I stroked its' wings and I noticed particularly, that it had a large, soft, domed head – exactly like Bozo. When I went back into the lounge later, the moth had gone and it hasn't appeared since.

To me, these two incidents with the moth were my sign – my message from Bozo that he had arrived safely and had said hello to

Jenna, Molly, Mole, Sweep (of course), Toni – Steve's Great Dane bitch that Bozo loved passionately, and no doubt Casey, Bomber and all our other beautiful lost hounds too. He let me know, as I'd asked him to, that he'd said hello to all of them, they're all together now and they're OK.

*(See photos, pages 65,68 &69)*

# Chelsea

Chelsea, (Alfie's sister), was Sweep's niece. Having succumbed to the third attack of Meningitis since the end of July last year ('04), she was put to sleep on Tuesday, June 14th. 2005.

She had been backwards and forwards to Liverpool Veterinary Hospital since the condition was first diagnosed and undergone operations and many months on steroids and numerous other drugs.

We had swum her regularly at a local Hydro-therapy pool in order to rebuild her wasted muscles and on June 6th, had taken her to Liverpool for what we hoped would be her last visit – which it turned out to be; though not for the reason we imagined.

They were amazed at the recovery she had made. She had regained all the weight previously lost when she was so terribly ill; the hair that had been shaved for the operations had re-grown and despite fears that she would never regain full use of one back leg; affected by the brain damage she suffered; she was strong and moving soundly.

She was almost weaned off all her medication and Liverpool signed her off.

It was the cruellest of blows, when less than a week later, she showed the first symptoms of Meningitis again.

We simply could not put her through any more suffering and so, she was put to sleep at home. She was just over seventeen months old.

******

There was no sign of, or from, Chelsea over the following months and though I knew that having passed over she would have been restored to health, I wondered if the brain damage she suffered might alter things and prevent her coming through.

*****

On Wednesday 21st. September, we were due to sail for Northern Ireland, for two Championship Shows. At 5.10am that morning, I was woken by Steve muttering and realised that he was enjoying a 'visit' from, I assumed, Sweep – which he was, but as it turned out, Sweep had brought practically the whole clan along with him. Steve had really hit the jackpot this time! There were so many details to remember about this visit, that I had to write them down as soon as I got up, to make sure I had them all correctly.

It was Molly who appeared first, or at least – her face did, grinning as she used to, with her lips drawn back to show all her teeth, (you would never mistake it for a snarl because she looked so funny), then her body appeared and quivered all the way along, ending in a tail wag. She always did that when she was excited.

Next, Mole appeared, at a gallop (no change there), followed by Sweep, who came for a fuss from Steve. Bozo appeared but stayed in the background, bounding about, then Jenna, who stood by the side of Molly.

At this point, Sweep ran off. Steve called him back but he wouldn't come - and then he came trotting back, very slowly, with Chelsea to his right hand side (left as you looked at them). At first her eyes were very wide and scary and her ears were pinned back against her neck but when she realised it was Steve, she came to him and slurped his arms.

Jenna stayed by Molly's side - still best friends  - and all of them appeared happy and well. Their surroundings were green and warm and Steve could make out other shadows in the background, though these were indistinct.

He described this 'dream' as having three dimensions. He was in the first and was unable to move forward into the second, (which was the dimension the dogs were in), but they could come to him. When they disappeared, it was into shadows in the third dimension. They didn't go into a mist; they were just not clearly defined anymore.

So, the family is together on the other side; they are happy and Chelsea is safe, because Sweep is looking after her.

*(See photo p.66)*

# *Slinky*

Slinky was Sweep's mother and Bozo's full sister. She had a history of skin problems, believed to be auto-immune related, was on medication for Hypothyroidism and then, as if that wasn't enough, she developed a bone-tumour on her right front-leg, which eventually, inevitably, grew so big that she had to be put to sleep.

The vet had told us that, as the tumour got bigger, the bone in the leg would get weaker and there was a strong possibility that the leg could break at any time, especially if she ran, or twisted it.

As she still behaved like a two-year old most of the time, we were very afraid that she was in real danger of ending her life in agony and so, we took the decision to have her put to sleep on a day when she was otherwise well and happy in herself, in order that she might have a peaceful and relatively pain-free end.

That day was Tuesday 25th October '05, just one month short of her eighth birthday.

I had given her a brush over in readiness and told her, as I had with Bozo, that it would soon be time for her to go to play with Bozo and Jenna, (their mother) and the others - including Sweep and Mole, her son and daughter of course. Again, as with Bozo, I asked if she would please let me know that she had arrived safely.

The vet came just before 1pm and luckily, Steve arrived home from work at the same time, so he was there to say goodbye to her as well.

*****

Later that afternoon, around 4pm, the phone rang and I went through to the kitchen to answer it. It was Gill, a friend of ours who also has Wolfhounds.

She knew about Slinky's leg and asked how she was. I told her that she had just been put to sleep.

'Oh, sorry; bad timing,' she said.

I assured her it was OK and was talking to her about why the decision was made and, as the phone is on the wall by the kitchen window, I was looking out of the window as we spoke.

Opposite the window is the end of the barn extension and its roof, at its lowest point, is at eye-level. There suddenly, from nowhere seemingly, (as I didn't see it appear – it wasn't there and then it was), just perched on the end of the guttering, was a bird, about the size of a thrush and the general colouring of a female blackbird (brown).

I didn't think too much of it at first but as I kept looking, I noticed that under its throat it had a faint mottled bib and then, as it turned, I saw white spots on its underside, not mottling like a thrush has but actual spots, about the size of a 5p coin, in amongst the brown feathers.

Gill must have realised that I was distracted because she asked what was wrong. I told her that a really strange bird had just appeared on the barn roof – and then it got stranger!

As I watched, it stretched its wings out very slowly, not flapping them and not attempting to fly away. The underside of the wings and all of its body (except for its back, which I couldn't see), were covered in the same white spots. It was as though someone had thrown ink onto blotting paper, only in reverse colouring - like the negative of a photograph.

Having displayed itself for several seconds, the bird folded its wings, walked up to the top of the barn roof and disappeared. It didn't fly off; it just disappeared.

I described all this to Gill as it happened and she had no more idea than I did what kind of bird it might be.

It was just the strangest thing. Not just the bird's markings but its behaviour. Eventually the thought came to me - this was my sign from Slinky, that she had arrived and was OK. She always was a strange old bird.

\*\*\*\*\*\*

I've described this bird to everyone I can think of that might know anything about birds.  I've looked on the RSPB's website and still I'm no nearer to knowing what it might be.  The only thing I can find with spots of any kind is a type of cuckoo - which would be very appropriate - Slinky was completely cuckoo, as anyone who ever knew her would tell you!

N.B.
If anyone *can* identify this bird, please let me know.  All I know is - I've never seen anything else like it, before or since.

*****

# Butterflies and Feathers

July 17th. 2006. I was in the barn, at the computer, working on the book. It was very hot and our new puppy, Molly (mark two), was lying flat out by the side of my chair. Suddenly, I experienced a poke in the midriff and turned immediately to see what Molly was doing. She was still flat out on the floor. Then I laughed and said, 'Hello Molls, happy birthday darling', because I realised I'd just had a visit from Molly (mark one) – and a reminder that July 17th  is the anniversary of her birthday. (I always remember, because it's the day after mine.)

Later the same morning, I was vacuuming in the barn and Molly puppy, who was standing at the other end of the barn, facing me, suddenly yelped and jumped forward with her back arched and her tail between her legs, as though something had touched and startled her. There was nothing there that I could see but I did wonder if Molly (mark one) was still about.

Later, when I moved into the passageway connecting the barn to the house and was vacuuming in there, there was a Red Admiral, wings folded, on the wall and a while later, in the bedroom, one appeared inside the Velux window.

Watching that one, it occurred to me that, although this year we've had lots of different kinds of butterflies about in the fields and the garden, some of which I've never seen before, the only ones we ever get indoors are Red Admirals. I wanted to add that observation to work in progress on the book, so headed back to the barn.

To be sure I wasn't imagining the fact, I made a point of asking Steve if he could ever remember any other sort of butterfly (not including moths), coming into the house and he said no, he couldn't. As I returned to the barn, there in the passageway connecting the barn to the house, were two tiny brown butterflies, flying round and round together! My first thought was – well, that's exploded that myth and made me a liar if I publish it.

Which of course it would but then I got to wondering whether there was some significance to those two tiny butterflies. I had more than a lump in my throat when I remembered that Molly (mark one) wasn't the only one whose birthday anniversary was 17th. July.

Two of her littermates, Lily and Oliver, were born with virus rhinitis and though I'd kept them and nursed them, they both caught pneumonia within a week of each other and were put to sleep on the same day, when they were just five months old.*

And as I was writing that, another butterfly appeared at the barn window, (I think it may have been a Painted Lady). It fluttered against the window for a long time.

When I went through to the kitchen later, there it was – wings spread out, inside on the kitchen windowsill. I couldn't believe it, another different kind of butterfly indoors, so I wondered who this sign was from.

I knew it must be someone I'd forgotten and I was almost ashamed when I remembered that July 17th was also Bomber's birthday, Molly's (and Lily and Oliver's) brother, who died when he was four years old, just two months after I moved to Wales.

So, eventually, thanks to the butterflies, they were all remembered, with love and fond memories, on the anniversary of their birthday.


*****


I had a feather experience too, that same day. I had parcelled up some things that Steve wanted posting and had left the parcel on the front edge of the dining table, which is also in the barn.

When I returned to the barn later on, there, right in the centre of the table, was a small white feather. There is nothing at all in the barn with feathers in it. The window at the rear of the barn and the Velux window were both open and the ceiling fan was going because it was so hot that day but the feather was behind the parcel when I found it, so logically, unless a freak gust of wind, (there was no breeze), had caught it outside and brought it in and then lifted it up over the top of the parcel and placed it, just by chance, exactly in the centre of the table, I just don't know how it got there, or where it came from.

Another of life's mysteries, except that, whenever I'm working in the barn, whatever I happen to be doing, it's never long before one or other of the dogs joins me!

\*\*\*\*\*

And  - a couple of days ago, just as I was about to step outside the front porch, I looked down and there, wings folded on the doormat, was a Red Admiral.  I said I didn't think the mat was a very sensible place for it to sit and put my finger down beside it, fully expecting it to fly off.  Instead, it climbed onto my finger and let me lift it up and carry it to the fence.  I tried to put it down onto a white throw that was drying on the fence but it wasn't having any of that and it flew off.  Are butterflies usually finger-tame?

*\*(See photo, p.70)*

\*\*\*\*\*

*Well,   -*

*for now at least, those are the visits*
*from our own dogs and the signs they have*
*sent for our reassurance   -  how much poorer*
*our lives would be if we hadn't recognised them.*

\*\*\*\*\*

# A Bridge Called Love

It takes us back to brighter years,
To happier sunlit days
And to precious moments
That will be with us always.

And these fond recollections
Are treasured in the heart
To bring us close to those
From whom we had to part.

There is a bridge of memories
From earth to Heaven above…
It keeps our dear ones near us
It's the bridge that we call love.


Author Unknown

# And
# so to
# your stories -

## Cynthia and Cimmie

*I**am beginning with this account, not only because it was the first
response I received from a reader of 'Over The Rainbow Bridge'
but because when I read it, my instinctive reaction was 'Wow, I
never thought I'd get one of these!' Cynthia e-mailed after reading
'OTRB', to share her life-saving experience -*

When I first read about your intentions to write this book, I didn't
send my experiences, as I had not actually seen my beloved one, only
felt her presence, albeit quite frequently, and still do, even now,
nearly eight years later.

Thankyou for writing 'Over The Rainbow Bridge', it has made me
feel so much better and it's good to know that I am not alone with
these feelings, however, when I read the part 'Contact Explained',
my jaw dropped open as realisation dawned and I now feel
compelled to write and tell you what happened to me. The contact
I'm talking about is Suicide Intervention, which, if it hadn't
happened, I wouldn't be here today.

*Cynthia goes on to explain -*

My favourite breed of dog is the Border Collie and my once-in-a-
lifetime dog was called Cimmie. Cimmie died at 10.30am on Boxing
Day 1996. I was so traumatised I couldn't function properly at all. I
felt my life had ended along with hers. I decided that I didn't want to
live in a world that didn't have Cimmie in it, so I planned my suicide,
so that I could go and be with her. But, before I could go through
with it, I had what I can only describe as a 'vision'. I wasn't asleep,
so it wasn't a dream; it was something I could see quite clearly.

This was my vision -

I had successfully committed suicide and gone to wherever we go to after death and there she was, my lovely Cimmie. She was happy, running and playing, (for some reason I can't explain, I've always thought she was reunited with her sister – I had never seen any of the other pups from the litter and don't even know if she had a sister – it was just something that came to me). I called and called her name but she just ignored me, or so I thought, until I saw that there was a huge thick pane of glass separating us and I realised that my punishment for killing myself, was never ever to be able to be with her; never to cuddle her and feel her beautiful fur and see her loving, trusting eyes looking into mine. I would have effectively cut myself off from her for all eternity and that was more unbearable than the pain of losing her. I knew then that I had to let my life take its natural course and that one day I will be with her again, this time forever. From that day, I have never thought of suicide again. I'm happy in the knowledge that one day we'll be together again.

Our bond was so strong, that even from the grave, Cimmie saved my life and my love for her has not diminished with the passing of time.

At the end of 'Over The Rainbow Bridge', you ask people to let you know of unusual happenings. For me it is a Robin. When we buried Cimmie, a Robin sat beside her grave and I said to myself, 'Every time I see a Robin I will think of her'. Sometime later, my daughter and I were visiting some gardens and as I walked along a path, a Robin was sitting on a post and we passed by quite close and even though I had a dog with me, the Robin showed no signs of flying away. It was as if he (or she) was waiting for me, so as we passed, I said 'Hi Cimmie, I still love you' and not until we had walked on did the Robin fly away. For me, these birds have become a symbol.

I'm sure that Cimmie comes with us on many of our walks as I quite often have the feeling that there is someone else with us and when I do a 'head count' to make sure all the dogs are where they should be, when I get to five, I feel sure I should then go on to say six and I also think she is visible to one of my Shelties who insists on lagging behind and when I stop to wait for her, she (the Sheltie), stops and looks behind her as if she is waiting for someone to catch up. I would love to think she is waiting for Cimmie.

*A friend told me that she had seen the following account on the Bone Cancer message board. I e-mailed Amy and she gave her permission for it to be included here.*

## Amy (USA) and Teddy

**The following is the original piece on the Bone Cancer message board -**

I had written to ask if anyone had experience with palliative radiation before I tried it with Teddy, my 12year old Airedale. It did work on his leg, however, there had to be cancer somewhere else. His pain became uncontrollable even with the heavy-duty pain meds.

I was so uncomfortable with euthanasia: how do you know when the time is right, and would it be OK with Teddy? I had the conversation with him several times about it being important to me that he be OK with euthanasia and that he needed to let me know when he was ready. I was absolutely not doing that without his OK.

I had a dream several days before we went to the euthanasia appointment, where I saw Teddy on his bed. He had many red lights (like miniature Christmas lights) all over him. I went to work the next day and told my boss about the dream. He said he thought the lights were all the places Teddy hurt.

A day later, my colleagues sent me home to be with Teddy, indicating they'd cover me (am I lucky or what: I love those guys!) That day, I went searching the web looking for info about when the time is right for euthanasia. I had so much doubt about my ability to determine the correct timing, or if there was correct timing. I had found something about the stages of death in animals and was reading it. I was here in the living room, and Teddy came running around the corner (running like O/S had never affected his leg!) He ran up to me, smiling and wagging his tail. I just looked at him and knew that he was ready and I had permission. That took a load off my shoulders. However, I was looking forward to more time with my goofy sweet guy.

He spent the afternoon outside in the sun (unusual in Michigan in winter).  By about seven o'clock that evening, he was panting and uncomfortable even with an extra pain pill.  I looked at him and asked him if he'd like to go be with Katie (July 2003 went to the Rainbow Bridge).  I told him if he wanted we could go see Dr. Froman and she'd give him a shot that would make all the pain go away: he'd go to sleep and he'd wake up and be with Katie.
Teddy could not get to the car fast enough: and so I called and asked if we could come in.  So we did.  And I cried (along with the vet techs who loved him too).
So, a couple of days after Teddy went to the bridge, I had a dream that he was lying on his bed.  He was covered with lights but they were now green.
I miss him and cry daily.  I think he's happy now and running again.

*After my e-mail, asking permission to use Teddy's story, Amy added the following in her reply -*

Teddy was a very vocal dog.  He always began to bark when he heard the alarm clock in the morning.  I am not a morning person, and this was reminiscent of growing up and hearing my Dad say, 'Amy, up and at 'em, rise and shine!'  Sometimes I got up just to make him stop.

Item one - The mornings between his euthanasia appointment, the evening of February 3, 2005 and the dream with the green lights, I heard him barking at me in the mornings.  This went on for several days until the green light dream.

Item two - This past weekend I dreamt that Teddy's lights were no longer green, but are now purple.  I got an e-mail from someone on the bone cancer site, several days after I posted, that indicated I may want to look into the significance of the colours and how they relate to spiritual transition.  To that end, I think the dreams are letting me know of his transformation from the physical, (red chakra), to the heart, (green chakra), to the spiritual, (purple).

# *Ann and Jack*

***Ann wrote to me after reading 'Over The Rainbow Bridge'. She says -***

My late, beloved Greyhound was called Jack. Having glued myself to the pages of your book until I'd finished, my time prior to and with, Jack, made even more sense than the conclusions I had already come to. I shall start at the beginning.

In 1999, having lost my job due to a back injury and being at home full time, we decided to get a retired Greyhound (as I had had one some years previously.) It had to me male, small and black. Why? Don't ask me, I just knew it did. Everywhere we went they were pleased we wanted a male but all were too big and none were black, and I would not be swayed. A trainer we had visited did, as a second thought, admit that she had heard of one that had just retired and gave me the trainer's name and number.

When we saw the dog, he was small and black but with a white throat, chest, paws and tail tip. I did not notice this but somehow it didn't matter. Although I didn't like his erect ears or the fact that he dismissed Mark and I as though we didn't exist, I said we'd take him. Why? I haven't got a clue. I just did.

The early days were traumatic for Jack (as I named him) and for myself and Mark. Jack would not settle and had to be with me at all costs. He wasn't all lovey-dovey, just didn't want to be left alone. In time, with lots of patience and understanding and many hugs and kisses, we became inseparable.

He was a strange dog, most unusual, not like any dog I've come across before. I often wondered if he was the reincarnation of a dog I hadn't understood many years earlier, or of some greater being – there was something great about him, as he humbled many people and dogs.

Some weeks after he first arrived, I wondered if he'd live as long as my previous Greyhound, (14 and a half years), but as soon as I thought that, an awful feeling went right through my stomach and I knew he'd never live to be old. At times, when I sat and stroked him and looked at his head, I knew something would go wrong in his head.

By May 2003 we had shared three and a half years with Jack, who was then 7 and a half. I had a 'message' from the spirit world (that's the only way I can think to describe it.)

On a Thursday, I had just returned from a coffee morning next door, which lasted an hour. I apologised to an upset Jack and told him, 'I'm going to get changed, then we'll go for our walk. I won't be long.' I went upstairs. While I was washing my hands, a voice, either in my head, or just by my head, (it was not an audible voice but telepathic, yet clear as anything), said, 'I'm going to take Jack.' I burst into tears and said, 'Don't take him, please don't take him.' Then I told myself not to be daft, I was imagining things. I wiped it from my memory, took Jack for his walk and didn't think about it again.

That evening Jack caught and ate a baby rabbit, whilst Mark was bringing the shopping in. Jack liked to show us when he'd caught a rabbit and I did feel a very slight feeling of disquiet but it wasn't much. When he finished his rabbit, he came indoors and wanted a hug from Mark, which was most unusual as he normally ignored Mark bringing in the shopping. Mark said he was too busy but I told him he must, as I could plainly see how important it was to Jack, so Mark knelt down and hugged him tightly for a while, which satisfied him.

The next evening, Friday, Jack suddenly became ill. He began vomiting and could not stop. We took him to the vets during the night. The first words I said were, 'If he dies, I want to take him home,' which surprised the vet greatly and me to an extent, as I certainly did not recall any of my premonitions at the time.

The vet said 'He's not going to die.' He gave him an anti-emetic but said that if Jack carried on being sick, then it was not his stomach but his brain (CNS) telling him to vomit. Jack carried on being sick and ended up on a drip. By Saturday night he was fitting, until a very severe fit rendered him brain-damaged. A new vet was on duty and had never seen a fit before.

Mark and I could not eat as our stomachs were in knots and our world was collapsing. We visited Jack as often as was possible, sat by his side talking to him and stroked his paws. One night I woke from a vision of Jack lying on his left side, not breathing. I shut this out too. By Tuesday morning, our vet said it was best to put him to sleep as his liver had broken down. I held Jack's head while Mark was close by and we both told him we loved him and said goodbye. When the nurse had removed all the drips, catheter and bandages, Jack was lying on his left side, as in my dream and it was something in his head that went wrong; his central nervous system had been attacked by a poison.

We took Jack's body home and put him in the kitchen while Mark dug a hole where Jack used to lie, by 'his bushes'. We placed food and water in the grave for his journey, closed the grave and planted a field maple before replacing the turf.

That evening, Mark and I decided to go on the same walk that he and Jack went every night, down to the church, through fields, as we live in a very rural area. It was Jack's favourite walk because of the rabbits. Just as we approached the gate to the church field, a Tawny Owl flew directly across our path, from left to right and hooted. This was unusual as the Tawnys were normally at the back of the house and we were at the front.

I told Mark that it was a message from the spirit world, to say that Jack had got there safely. To some Native Americans, owls are messengers from the spirit world.

Three days after we buried Jack, we both smelt an anaesthetic and urine aroma, which was how Jack smelt when we removed him from the plastic bag we'd brought him home in from the vets. The smell was just inside the living room door, where Jack used to lie watching us in the kitchen. We knew it wasn't from the bag itself, as that was only put in the kitchen and the kitchen didn't smell. We could only assume that it was Jack.

Over the next two weeks, at different times, I smelt the same smell in various parts of the house. It would last a few seconds. Mark also smelt Jack around the house and I smelt him twice on a walk in the woods. In that same two weeks, I met a dog-walker who had known Jack. She had her two Yorkies, plus a Labrador bitch and a Golden Retriever bitch with her. The Retriever had always barked at Jack, all bluster - no malice, as she quite liked him really.

This particular day, as we stood on a woodland track and I explained about Jack's death, her Retriever, who was standing ahead of me, suddenly started barking and looking further up the track but no one was there.

I said 'It must be Jack'. He always stood at a distance waiting for me. I could just imagine him standing sideways on, looking at me.

After those two weeks we went on holiday to Cornwall. I was dreading going at this time. Jack hated travelling and I knew, even in spirit, he probably wouldn't come with us. It was an awful week. The scenery was lovely and the weather was quite good but I lay sobbing in bed every night, as I missed Jack so much.

When we set off for home I instantly felt calmer and once at home I just knew Jack was with me. A day or two later, while sitting in the kitchen taking my Wellingtons off, I smelt a strong scent of my dad, who died in 1999, just before we got Jack. I knew it was him as he had a unique smell. I felt he was saying 'It's all right, Jack's with me. He's fine.'

A month after Jack's passing, due to pressure from others and confusion on our part, we went to the local re-homing kennels for the nearest Greyhound stadium. Strangely, most of the dogs were small black males, yet when we were searching previously, Jack was the only one. We brought a brindle dog home.

It was evening, so there was not much time to settle him in before bedtime. The new dog refused to get into Jack's bed, so I put Jack's old duvet in the opposite corner of the room and the dog lay down. I slept on the settee to keep him company but broke down in floods of tears. I knew it wasn't right, this dog was not meant for us; he had to go back.

Sadly we returned him. I had intended to call him Charlie. Six months later I found out that he now has a lovely home with a retired couple who knew Jack. He's now called Charka – spookily close to Charlie! I couldn't help wondering if Jack was in his bed and wouldn't let Charlie/Charka in.

By September 2003 I had begun writing a book about Jack. In October, Mark and I went for our usual week to a small, coastal village in North Wales. Jack had been there with us a few times. I felt he was with us and was quite happy, until half way through the week. I woke one morning and knew he'd gone back home. I said to Mark, 'Jack's gone back. I don't want to stay. I'd like to go home and carry on with my book.'

Mark didn't mind and once home I felt Jack's presence. He has remained with me to this day and on occasions he still lets me know by leaving that anaesthetic/urine scent, especially after reading 'Over The Rainbow Bridge'. I also smelt him a couple of times before we went to a Greyhound gala to sell my book. His basket occasionally creaks and as it stands on a concrete floor it is not through floor movement. I wonder if it is Jack and say 'hello' to him, just in case.

Having smelt Jack and then my dad, I thought back to after my mum died in March 2000. I smelt her twice, in our bedroom here in Norfolk, where she'd never been in her life. At the time I dismissed it as imagination but I now believe that it was her 'visiting' me.

Also, after watching a Kilroy programme, some time after Jack's passing, about mediums and guardian angels and spirit guides, I went for my walk as usual and at one point in the walk, I felt someone just behind and to my left, then a weight on my shoulders. I kept looking round but no one was there. You know when someone stands right near you? They don't have to touch you but you know they're there. I wondered if it was a spirit guide putting an arm round my shoulders, or perhaps my mum or dad.

It's strange how I was able to forget all the premonitions until a few days after Jack's death. Or was I meant to forget? I know that remembering again has really helped me to accept Jack's going, as I now know it was meant to happen that way. I feel I was chosen (or both Mark and I), to share some of Jack's life, that's why I was guided to a small, black male and there was only one available at the time.

Another thing that struck me afterwards, was Jack's wanting Mark to hug him when he was bringing the shopping in. It made me think back to the last time I saw my mum before she died. We were leaving after a visit and she waved madly from her bedroom window and blew kisses; something she definitely never did normally. I felt strange and upset leaving and she died a few days later.

I think that, when loved ones are getting near their passing, they subconsciously want to be closer to you. Whether it is their soul saying goodbye, or letting you know they love you, or someone from the spirit world instructing them without them realising of course, I don't know.

Who on earth told me 'I'm going to take Jack'?   Who has the power to take souls?   Are premonitions messages from the spirit world?  I will only truly find out when it's my turn to join Jack and I know he'll meet me at the door.  I look forward to going home.

*****

*(See photo, page 75)*

# Catherine and Bugsy

### Catherine sent a very moving e-mail after reading 'OTRB' -

Thankyou so very much for 'Over The Rainbow Bridge'. It arrived yesterday and I read it last evening in one sitting, I could not put it down. I simply cannot tell you just how much comfort it brought me.

I have had many dogs during my life, all loved beyond reason. Bugsy, a Shar Pei, came into my life by default, in 1989. I had his litter sister and his breeder rang me, telling me her litter brother needed to be rehomed, as he simply did not get along with the family's other dog. Bugsy arrived in my home and walked right into my heart. He was less than two years old.

When he was almost four years old, he suddenly became very ill. He died unexpectedly at the vets, while undergoing treatment. I was devastated. I had other dogs of course, so had to keep 'going through the motions'.

Three days after his death, I was preparing the dogs' evening meal, tears rolling down my face, when I suddenly heard the sound only Bugsy made when excited; a kind of 'yip'.

I turned round and there he stood, grinning at me in the old way, wagging his tail.

I must have been frozen to the spot for a moment but managed to speak to him. He continued to wag his tail for a moment and then he was gone. It never happened again and nothing similar has happened, either before, or since.

I convinced myself it was imagination but having read your book, I now believe Bugsy came to tell me all was well and to say goodbye.

As I write, I can now picture the beauty of the Rainbow Bridge, where all my lost companions are waiting for me to join them. The gift you have given me is immense; I quite simply do not have the words to adequately express my gratitude.

For the moment, the tears are flowing again, this time though perhaps, with relief, knowing for certain that I can look forward to seeing all my darlings again.

# Elizabeth , Adrian and the Borzois

*Elizabeth wrote after reading 'OTRB'. The wording of her first paragraph is typical of that in so many of the letters I have received – the knowledge now, that others have had similar experiences and the comfort that knowledge brings.*

I want to thank you from myself and my husband for sharing your experiences with us and sharing the knowledge that we are not alone in what we have experienced over the past few years.

Our heartache started in May 2001, when we lost our beloved Borzoi boy, Zak, to cancer, at the age of eight years. He was one of the first (and only) litter we ever bred; deciding to keep half of the litter – too soft I guess!

Two months after losing Zak, in July 2001 we lost his brother, our lovely Ringo, to a brain tumour, just after his ninth birthday. Then, four months later, in November, we lost their father, Zari, (Bunnyboy); to old age I guess – he was eleven.

We were left with two siblings, our beloved Dimitri and Sable, the last of our dogs, and line.

We had our hearts thoroughly torn to pieces over this year and realised, with crushing reality, that they were no longer the beautiful bottle fed, (their mother had mastitis), babies we had hand-reared and nursed, but that they had grown old and no-one had told us.

Even now, the pain in my heart and throat as I write, is truly crushing and very painful. From the time of losing Zak, we have been visited by Red Admiral butterflies, usually in our bedroom, first one, then of course, when Ringo and Zari were lost, we had three that seemed to take up permanent residence in our bedroom, throughout the winter, over our bed. Though we did not know until reading your book, that they were indeed significant, even at the time, we 'knew' they were important. We treated them with respect and enjoyed their presence.

Also, the noises. So many times, hearing thuds upstairs when we were all downstairs, to the point where we began to leave bedroom doors open – for ease of access for whoever might have been there?!

(Sorry, but we've never discussed any of this with anyone other than ourselves, - the usual story of people just wouldn't understand.)

Shortly after we lost Ringo we were visited by a very beautiful blackbird. Ringo was a beautiful deep blue-black colour – a real stunner. And this bird was no different. Never seen before, he would sit in our garden and quite literally stare into the living-room, making no attempt to move, even when we went outside; strange for an unknown, wild, blackbird.

I even took to asking him if he was my Ringo coming to see me.

Anyway, after much searching and heartache, we bought a new puppy, a little girl – Anoushka – who we hoped to breed from in time, and a new friend for Sable and Dimitri.

But, in July 2002, tragedy struck again, and my beautiful Dimitri had to leave. He truly was my soulmate, my closest companion. He had seen me through so many difficulties and he never, ever, left my side.

He knew whenever I was on my way home and would go to the door ten minutes before I arrived, allowing my husband time to put the kettle on. From the time I met my husband, (who was smitten with these beautiful hounds at first sight), he remarked on the amazing bond that he both saw and felt between myself and Dimitri, who would gaze longingly into my eyes and I would 'know' what he wanted. We always seemed to sense what the other was thinking. God, how I miss him.

Anyway, I lived in a daze afterwards and I know my husband became very concerned and arranged to find another puppy – something I had no interest in at the time.

We found Vaziliy at the end of August. He was a tiny, six weeks old bag of bones.

I won't go into the state he was in, or the anger I feel towards his breeder, but the moment I saw him, the mothering instinct was there and he was the best therapy. He needed me – and I needed him. The strange thing is, that he was born ten years, to the exact date, after my Dimitri's birthday.

He is identical in colour and has very similar markings. He is not my boy, I know that, but the bond is there. He is my baby, - my husband often remarks on his behaviour with me.

He would insist on me carrying him upstairs to bed every evening
– pushing into me and 'sitting' in my arms, as natural as anything,
though no-one else could even attempt to pick him up, he would
become rigid and very heavy.

Now, even though he is almost two years old, and growing to be a
very fine young man, whenever I put my arms in front of him, he will
shift into position and become light as a feather and I can carry him
with ease, he is so light. Yet my husband struggles to pick him up –
he says he is so heavy now!

Anyway, I had experiences of songs on the radio – songs directly
relating to the dogs in various ways, and the feeling (the insight) of
Dimitri in the car, even though he was gone.

We thought then, going into winter, with Sable the matriarch, and
our two youngsters, that we might have a little relief.  But,
horrendously, in February 2003, a week after my husband's birthday,
we lost Anoushka, - not even fifteen months old.

Now this is hard.  She was to my husband, as Dimitri had been to
me. And God, how I wished the earth had opened up and taken us all.

We had no chance to say goodbye.  Our world collapsed. Vazi was
devastated, they were best friends, inseparable.  He looked
everywhere for her and took to sitting on the floor, sucking and
kneading their favourite teddy bear toy. Heartbreaking. My husband
was lost and I was angry that they took her so young.

My husband has felt her nudging him whilst at work.  Also, one
day, again at work, he had a small white feather flutter down on him.
He works in a spotless, lazer engineering business and knew it could
only be from her.  He is upset still that he did not keep it safe – and it
seemed to disappear.

We have both 'smelt' our dogs, but never seen them unfortunately.
We put our house on the market in the summer but received a call
from Anoushka's breeder to say she wanted us to have a puppy she
had just bred, which had been destined for America, but she would
rather we had.

We met her at six weeks (with all the litter) and she 'chose' us.
She made a bee-line for my husband and drank from his glass (it was
pink grapefruit juice!). He was smitten and slowly his heart began to
heal. The nudging from Anouchka stopped.

The butterflies moved on (even though it was summer). We had collected 'Lular', (otherwise known as Pig and Woodpecker, but only when said in a Norwegian voice), on the 26th. July 2003, - one year exactly to the day we had lost Dimitri, and two years to the day of our wedding.

We moved house and in the winter the butterflies arrived, for a brief period, and then left. We haven't seen any since.

Last month we had to say goodbye to the grand lady Sable, who - throughout everything, was a rock. She was just short of her twelfth birthday.

But she had aged a great deal in recent months – as though time had run to keep up, and hers was a peaceful departure, gone to put some law and order to her brothers and father, and Anoushka.

Strangely, losing her, though upsetting, was not like losing the others, perhaps because we'd been expecting it for some time, I don't know.

We have felt so much guilt over this past three years, regret, pain, everything. Always questioning, if only? What if? Should we have? Beating ourselves up time and again. We cherish our babies everyday, they truly are our world – in this life.

We both look forward to the day that we can all be re-united. We've both had some very strange, ethereal dreams, upsetting and comforting; the sand on the beach, the dogs running free – blurring into the distance. Loss on waking, that feeling of needing to get back to that place – to be near them, to smell them again.

### *Elizabeth finished by saying -*

Thankyou, for letting me tell someone else, to share with someone I know will understand. Thankyou for your book, thankyou for the hope.

*****

## Elizabeth (America) and Cinder

**Elizabeth had sent for a copy of 'Over The Rainbow Bridge' and e-mailed to let me know that the book had arrived safely. She said -**

It is a very interesting new way to look at Rainbow Bridge. I am now listening carefully for my fur kids that have crossed. I am sure now that my grandfather stayed with me for some time when he passed years ago and that when my heartdog, Cinder, crossed, she visited me for sometime, as a single Monarch butterfly would pass through the yard as I was feeling sad about it. This happened for a little while and they have never been back. I didn't recognize what was happening then but I knew my heart lifted for a little while.
Thankyou,
Elizabeth.

*****

*My beautiful Bozo. See page 33.*

*Chelsea (foreground) and Alfie, approx. 3 months old. See page 38.*

*Sweep. See page 27.*

*Close-up of Bozo's moth, (bottom left-hand corner), on Sweep's photo. See page 35.*

*The pictures on the wall behind my chair. See page 36.*
*Time 9.40 pm (see clock) Bozo's moth ringed.*

*Lily & Oliver, See page 44.*

*Darling Molly, See page 24.*

*Orbs In The Barn. 4th. October '04. See page.29.*

*Oliver. Marguerite's Pewter Persian cat. See page 123.*

*Patricia's Diesel. See page 134.*

*Ann's Greyhound, Jack. See page 53.*

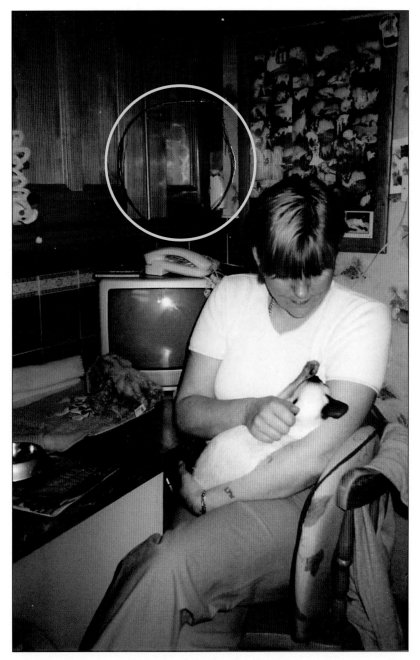

*Lynda and Omaya, being watched over by Oreo. See page 119.*

*Shirley and Kev's Irish Wolfhound, Jud, enjoying his first visit to the beach. See page 147.*

*Amanda and Tia. See page 158*
*Mutual Love*

*Tia waving. See page 158.*

*'OLAF' Willeke's Wolfhound, 'wearing of the green' on St. Patrick's Day. See page 155.*

*The story of Bridgette (page 88 'OTRB'), describes how her owner, Brenda, saw her in the clouds after her death. Brenda said, 'she looked happy, almost smiling but she appeared to have wings and a unicorn horn'. I wondered about the wings and the unicorn horn, until, long after 'OTRB' was published, I found the following extract in one of my books, I won't say 'quite by chance', because you must realise by now, I believe nothing happens just by chance - or coincidence. The book is a real life story.*

*Extract from 'Wild Stone Heart', An Apprentice In The Fields, by Sharon Butala.*

'That day the view through the windshield was of low, fat clouds, blue and mauve-tinted, with rounded, charcoal bottoms. There was a wind blowing across the highway from north to south, and it might soon begin to rain. I saw all this, felt it, did not think about it. I was for the moment a creature of the road and of the landscape; it was there and so was I. An antelope came up out of the ditch on my left and I braked. I'd only been going about fifty miles per hour, thinking, there he is again, I wonder where his partner is; he crossed the road on an angle in front of me, moving fast as antelope do, and – how beautiful antelope are – I watched him run down into the ditch on the other side and up onto the farmland where he stopped, turned, and faced me, waiting. As he ran down into the ditch, I saw first his white rump and then the wind rippling his short black mane, and a small delight grew in me, low in my abdomen.

I pushed on the gas and drove on, perhaps ten feet, when suddenly a shock went through me. *What was that?* I rehearsed what I had just seen: how the clouds had parted narrowly and beams of white light shone down on the road in front of me and the antelope, how his body turned slightly away from me, his head lifted, and a wide beam of bluish white light bathed him, in it his warm-brown body turned a hazy blue-white and – *he became a unicorn.*

I think I laughed. I drove on, my whole viscera open, in awe, in amazement, in joy. My chest did something funny, I'm not sure what. It opened up; it melded into my breath. I think, for some minuscule portion of time, I thought I could fly. But I didn't, I drove on to Shaunavon. And I didn't tell anyone. Not for months. But I did not – I do not – doubt what I saw. And I knew, too, not that I understood then or that I understand even now, that what had happened was that my eyes had opened to *see what is always there*.

In that instant the "real" world had cracked and split narrowly apart – "a veil shimmered apart and there he was in another light, white world," my journal says – and I was allowed a glimpse of the mythic world we're told exists right beside or behind, or maybe inside, the "real" one'......

\*\*\*\*\*

# Glynis and Vixen

*The following is taken from Glynis' letter, about Vixen – her Red Point Siamese cat -*

Vixen was not my first choice from the litter – it was a partnership that really had no beginning, not even love at first sight. To put it bluntly, I had no desire to have a 'Red Point' Siamese and could honestly state a distinct dislike for the colour.

I had specifically stressed to the breeder, that I wanted a 'Lilac Point', of which there was only one, a very weak, weedy kitten and against the breeder's protests, I was determined to purchase it. I totally ignored the bold, strong, red point kitten.

The breeder's words came true and after less than a week, my little lilac point kitten passed away.

The breeder was also upset and arrived at my home with 'Vixen', the red point, as a replacement.

It was a relationship that neither Vixen, nor myself, looked forward to but she became one of the most fascinating Siamese cats I ever owned.

Through the years, I marvelled at her communication skills. I endured a horrific divorce, including vast upset. Vixen read my moods and made it her prime job in life to be my comfort.

If her food tray was empty, she would jump on my lap and put her paw on my lips – not scratching but urging me to get up. She always curled up on my shoulder if I was ever crying and pawed at my tears.

In fact two became one – and we adored each other.

At over twelve years old, when we moved house Vixen travelled with us, always loose, curled up with the dogs – she couldn't abide cat carriers.

Tragically, within a couple of months, Vixen met her end after being hit by a car. She had been searching for me, as I had returned to the house, forgetting my phone.

I at least managed to pick her up while she was still warm and sob my last goodbyes to a well loved friend, knowing for sure I'd lost a piece of my heart.

We buried her in a special place in the garden and her loss was everywhere to me, in everything I did.

The following evening, sitting in our front room, I said to my husband, 'Open the door, Vixen's calling outside to come in'.    I could hear her well known cry to open the door, never once registering the fact that she was no longer with us.

My husband reminded me of her death and I said, 'Listen, she's out there.' I opened the door and the crying ceased.

A couple of nights later, I got up in the early hours to go to the bathroom and still a little bit hazy about finding my way around in the dark at our new home, I put on the lights.  On the return trip, I walked through the front room and saw Vixen, curled up asleep on the chair, on what was her usual cushion and sheepskin.  I remember thinking fleetingly – good, the cat's in.  I entered the bedroom and then reality hit me when I suddenly remembered her death.   I immediately opened the bedroom door and looked at the chair – she was no longer there.   I woke my husband who told me I was dreaming but, I have trouble sleeping normally, having done twelve years of night shifts – I certainly hadn't dreamt it!

After losing Vixen, I was given a common little moggy kitten, (although a pretty grey/blue tabby, my heart belongs to Siamese). We called it 'Mittens' and I told it from day one, it could never fill the large gap in my life since Vixen.

I was amazed that within a week, this little kitten had re-enacted all Vixen's habits, including pawing at my lips and curling on my shoulder.  I had taught it none of these actions.  Mittens now follows me everywhere, sits on my lap as soon as I enter the front room and uses the same cushion to sleep on as Vixen did.

I can't explain what I feel when I look in the kitten's eyes but there's a kind of knowing that passes between us.

Maybe I'm just a sentimental softie, or maybe Vixen has provided me with a comfort – but I've neither heard from, nor seen her anymore since the arrival of Mittens.

# Helen – Gt. Danes

*Helen is a treasurer for Gt Dane Rescue. The story of her Great Dane 'Elijah', appeared in 'OTRB'. She rang me to tell me about a feather experience she'd had. In her own words -*

Spring 2004. I am an early riser, getting up at 4.30am every morning to start work. The morning in question, I had seen to my dogs and was doing my usual housework. It was a very cold, windy, wintry day and so, all the doors and windows were closed.

My house has polished wooden floors downstairs and I had moved all the chairs and other furniture, given everywhere a thorough vacuuming until it was all spic and span, then replaced all the furniture and having had a good look round to make sure everything was OK, had gone upstairs for a nap.

When I came downstairs, the first thing I noticed was a small white feather, in front of the chair where I usually sit. It was in exactly the place where my feet would rest if I were sitting down and I'm absolutely sure it wasn't there when I finished cleaning. With all the doors and windows closed there were no draughts that could have blown it in from outside, I have no feather cushions or anything else with feathers in it and I have absolutely no idea where it could have come from.

\*\*\*\*\*\*

*The following accounts are taken from Janet's letters and relate
some of her many experiences, both with her own departed hounds
– and others -*

# Janet and her Wolfhounds

*Janet writes -*

**Gersha** was an Irish Wolfhound bitch, which I acquired in a very
neglected state, through an ad in a local paper.  Purely by chance,
through taking her to a Wolfhound rally, someone recognised her
name, which hadn't been changed and told me that Gersha was the
mother of their dog and that she was about eight years old.  She lived
with me for three years but due to a bad heart, in May 1985 she had
to be put to sleep.

At the time, I had two other, male, Wolfhounds, Mahoney and
Bevis.

About two weeks after Gersha was put to sleep, I went out
shopping and was returning home, laden with bags, when, as I
approached my front door, (my only thought at that time being a cup
of tea and a cigarette), a feeling of tremendous peace flooded over
me and at the same time, I had a vision of a meadow with long
grasses and wild flowers.  It was as though I was seeing everything
through Gersha's eyes.  She was standing at the bottom of a small
rise with a wood at the top and was surrounded by other Wolfhounds.
The message seemed to be that she was happy and content.

Strangely, in 1991, Michael Ellis had an article printed in the
Wolfhound Magazine.  His wife had seen the same type of flower-
strewn meadow with lots of Wolfhounds - she had seen this in a
dream.  I have never met or spoken to the Ellis's.

*****

One day in the summer of that year, I was mixing food for Mahoney
and Bevis when Gersha pushed herself between me and the work-
surface and I instinctively moved aside to let her squeeze past into
the back yard.  Then, I suddenly realised what had happened - that

Gersha was no longer with us - and looked into the yard to see if she was still there.

From where I was standing at the time, there appeared to be great sunlight shining in through the open door; very, very bright. When I got to the door, the yard was actually in shade and rather dull, as the sun was at the front of the house at that time of day.

*****

**Mahoney** was the next to leave, on 4th. June 1987. On the night he died, everything was fine at 5p.m. but by 10p.m., he had gone. I still find it too painful to talk about the circumstances surrounding his death but it left me feeling very guilty and as though I'd let him down. I prayed and prayed for forgiveness, until one night I had a dream in which I felt Mahoney snuggle against my left hip and push his head up under my left arm, as if he was telling me that everything was alright.

Some while after, my daughter and I went to a Spiritualist meeting. The Spiritualist said that she felt I had been asking someone for forgiveness and they wanted me to know that I had been forgiven. The Spiritualist told me how this 'person' had come to her in a dream.

*****

**Bevis.** On Friday 29th December 1989, around 7.15a.m, Bevis died of pneumonia, brought on by Kennel Cough.

He always used to lie at the foot of the stairs and would lie down in a series of thuds, shaking the floorboards in the process. At 9.40p.m on New Years' Eve, my mother and I were watching television when we both heard that familiar noise and, at the same time, felt the floorboards vibrate. We both shot to the door to look but no-one was there.

On the Thursday evening, about 6p.m, the same thing happened and this time, my brother was there and he heard it too but again, when we looked, no-one was there.

At 7a.m, on the following Friday, I had done all my early morning jobs and was ready to take Jacob out for his walk, when I heard a tap on the door, then another; in the way Mahoney used to hit the door with his paw when he wanted in; then an impatient raking of claws down the door – exactly what Mahoney would have done – and I just knew it must be him. I opened the door - only to find nothing there. From that time on, I didn't hear Bevis again and I think Mahoney came for him. There had been a lot of unusual activity in the house up until then, especially the sound of doors slamming, (even ones that were locked) but it all stopped from that time on, as though Bevis, in spirit, had chased everything away. He had always been a sensible guard.

Some months after Bevis died, I had fallen asleep in the early afternoon and on waking was dumbfounded to see, through the window, his face in perfect detail in cloud formation. The sky was blue with just some fluffy cloud about. On this particular occasion I hadn't been thinking about Bevis and could think of no reason why he should suddenly appear, except to give me comfort.

There were however, many other times when I did think about him and want him to be back with me. One night I had a vivid dream. I was walking with him along a high ridge. Lower down I could see and hear children laughing and playing in a playground and other people in the distance. There was a happy holiday atmosphere. The message that was coming across to me was, 'I'm happy here – please leave me be.'

*****

**Jacob** was another of my Wolfhounds. I had him as a ten-week-old puppy, in 1987. He was put to sleep on 31st. January 1994, at 6 and a half years of age. He had had Rhinitis and septicaemia. The vet had been treating him but his legs, particularly one hind leg, had swollen very badly. It was as though all his old ailments had returned and the night before he died he was in a great deal of pain. I gave him Homeopathic Arsen Alb, in high potency, to calm him and to ease his death when it came and I tried but failed to get hold of my vet, eventually managing to contact him at 8a.m the following morning. It was 10a.m before he arrived.

Meanwhile, Jacob had calmed down. I had been praying throughout the night for Mahoney and Bevis to come and fetch him, to be there to greet him as he died. (I felt he shouldn't go alone – because knowing Jacob he would get into all sorts of trouble.)

The vet arrived with a nurse and I knelt on the floor with Jacob's head resting on my left forearm. Just as the vet was giving him the injection to put him to sleep, he lifted his head right up and turned to look at the armchair behind him across the room; staring intently at it, as though someone was there; so much so that the vet and the nurse turned to look too.

At that very instant, I heard a voice in my head saying 'He's mine and he's coming with me.' It was a woman's voice and the woman was obviously very angry, though I had no idea why, as I always loved Jacob and looked after him well, although I somehow always had the feeling that he wasn't mine.

Some time after, whilst reading a poem I had been sent, about Jacob being free as the wind on the other side, I felt the gentlest of breezes waft across my face. There were no windows or doors open that could have caused this to happen.

\*\*\*\*\*

My father had a cat named Amber, who became gravely ill with cancer. My father had been terribly distressed at having Amber's older companion put to sleep three or four years before and couldn't bear the thought of taking Amber to the vet's to have him put to sleep also. I was upset to see the cat so ill. I knew that Amber was dying and prayed for someone to be there to meet him when he died.

A week or so later, I was asleep, when I half woke to feel a cat materialising on my stomach. I could feel it lying down with its front paws curled under its chest. For a moment I thought it must be Amber, that he'd died but in fact he hadn't, he died two days later. The night he was dying he was restless and fidgety, so I gave him Homeopathic Arsen Alb. He became settled, fell asleep and died peacefully the following morning, giving one last mew before he went.

I now feel that the cat I felt on my stomach was perhaps my father's other cat and Amber's companion, Tic Tac, who was put to sleep previously and that my prayers had been answered and he had come for Amber.

*****

Friends of mine had a German Shepherd Dog called Ted. They often accompanied my dogs and me on our walks. One day, while Bevis was still alive, on the way home from the park, I had taken a detour down a road that we didn't normally use and stopped at the butcher's for some bones.

All the way home Bevis was trying hard to get the bones from the bag and after that he always wanted to go that way home.

I feel that Ted must have had a special connection with Bevis. Two things in particular happened to make me think that way. The first was three days after Bevis died.

I was out with Jacob when I saw my friends out with Ted. Ted charged towards me, looking towards my left side but when he reached me he stopped and looked totally confused. I wonder if perhaps he'd seen Bevis walking with me.

A week after Bevis died, my friends and I were out walking with Jacob and Ted, when Ted started pulling to go down the road to the butcher's, something that he hadn't done before. He was staring intently down the road and we all looked hard to see what he was staring at. We spotted a carrier bag caught on something and being blown by the wind and thought it must be that but we realised he was looking straight past it. Eventually we came to the conclusion that he must have seen Bevis.

I wondered if Bevis was perhaps still trying to get me to go that way.

Ted was obviously a very intuitive dog. Often when my friends and I were out walking we would see a husband and wife out with their two Borzois; the husband walking in front with one, the wife following behind with the other.

After one dog died, the husband and wife walked together with the remaining one. Whenever Ted saw them he would bark frantically but would be looking behind them. We eventually came to the conclusion that he must be seeing and barking at the dog that had been put to sleep. (I found out later that that was the dog that the wife used to walk, behind the other one.) It had always been Ted's habit to bark at it when it was alive. Its owners were very comforted by Ted's behaviour - after their dog had died that is!

\*\*\*\*\*

My present Wolfhound is Willum. He is now ten years old and I have had him since he was a puppy. From twelve weeks of age he seems to have been aware of his predecessors.

I remember one day in particular when Willum started barking at something across the room. The height his eyes were fixed on would have been at about the same height as a Wolfhound head when it was lying down resting on its elbows. Willum shot behind my legs and bravely continued his barking while peeping out from his hiding place. This continued for a minute or so before he stopped. He never did it again.

On the 16th anniversary of Mahoney's death, Willum was lying down in the hall, when he suddenly shot up, rushed into the room and spun round. He stared out of the door intently, and although there was nothing there as far as I could see, I feel that it could have been Mahoney visiting. This went on for three nights, always at around the same time.

When Willum was still a young dog and I used to walk him in the park, we always seemed to arrive there at the same time as a woman with a crossbreed dog called Tigger. Whenever Tigger saw us he would fly across at Willum and attack him. Although I tried hard to avoid the times when I thought the woman would be there, it seemed that she was trying to do the same thing, because whatever time we arrived, she and Tigger would arrive too.

By the time Willum was fourteen months old he'd had enough and one day when Tigger ran at him, Willum grabbed him by the back of the neck and shook him. He came to realise that if he charged first, then Tigger ran off.

At first he confined this defensive tactic to Tigger but eventually he would run at any dog he saw, not to attack but just to frighten them away, though I was always afraid that one day it would result in bloodshed.  I tried changing to a different park for our walks and although this worked at first, before long Willum started chasing other dogs again.

One day, when Willum had set off after a dog, I was so afraid of the outcome that I prayed to Mahoney and Bevis to please stop him. Willum immediately slowed down and came back to me.  Every time it happened after that, I prayed and Willum slowed down and came back.  He eventually regained his confidence in other dogs.

***Sadly, sometime after receiving Janet's first letter, she wrote to let me know that Willum had had to be put to sleep.  The following is taken from her second letter -***

For the few days prior to Willum being put to sleep, knowing that the end was coming, I had been asking for somebody that he had known in life to come and meet him.  I was concerned though, that as he had never willingly gone anywhere unless I went too, that he may not go with whoever came to meet him, not even Mahoney and Bevis, who I was convinced he had known, or at least, had been aware of sometimes being there, because of his response in stopping his charging at strange dogs.

We were waiting for the vet's last visit.  Willum was lying quietly, not having moved at all since he had been cleaned up and made as comfortable as possible.  I was sitting with him, and still asking, in my mind, that someone would come to meet him.  The door to the hall was open and the sun was shining in at the doorway.

Suddenly Willum lifted his head and looked towards the door.  He pricked his ears and continued to look.  I could see nothing unusual and there were no sounds from outside that I could hear.  After a few moments he put his head down and didn't move again, not even when I showed the vet and his nurse in.

It was a Wednesday when Willum was put to sleep.  The following Sunday evening, I was alone watching television.  Although I was watching the programme, Willum was constantly in my thoughts. Near the end of the programme I noticed a smell that I associated with him when he was ill. Rather faint at first, it steadily got stronger. At first it registered as Willum but then I remembered that of course, he was no longer there. The smell persisted for a little while, then seemed to get even stronger. After a while it faded.

The following evening at around the same time, the smell came back again, this time getting so strong that it was in the back of my throat. This was in the room where Willum had been put to sleep and not the room I had been in the evening before.

I was concerned. What, if anything, did this smell mean? Had Willum not gone, was he stuck here, indeed, was he still ill and in pain?

I felt sure someone had come for him, by his looking at the door as though his name had been called. Was he still behaving as he did in life and being unwilling to go anywhere without me?

The following morning, still pondering whether there was a problem or not, I decided to pray for/call on, his mother, Naomi, to come for him. I told her he was messing around and perhaps she could talk some sense into him. I imagined her saying something to him along the lines of 'Now come on son, stop mucking about, you can't hang around here. You'll only get ignored anyway, she can't see you, however much she would want to.' Coincidence or not, the smell has never returned.

I came down one morning two or three weeks after Willum died, to find a feather dead centre of my computer keyboard (where I spend a lot of time). Smallish, about two inches long but it was a dirty grey and then brownish at the base. It wasn't there when I'd gone to bed. There's nothing in the room with feathers in, no feather filled cushions or anything. So how did it get there? And grey? Is the colour significant, do you think?

A month to the day after Willum was put to sleep, it was in the early hours of the morning and I couldn't sleep. I was beset by worries of what I had, or hadn't done for him. Could I have done more? Did I do the right things? All the usual feelings that come with grieving. More tossing and turning. To cap it all, although the alarm was set for 5am, the time shown was erratic, as I discovered from my frequent checking of the clock. The batteries were wearing down. Was it time to get up? Would I overstay in bed? I've always liked to be up early, feeling the day was out of kilter if I overslept. Equally, I didn't want to get up too early, what was the point, it offered no peace from those churning thoughts. More tossing and turning.

Then I heard Willum whine, just once, at the foot of the stairs. Instinctively, I began to get up to let him out for a wee, as I'd always done and then realised what I was doing. Nevertheless, I was out of bed, dressed and downstairs in a trice. Nothing there.

The clock in the morning room showed it was exactly 5am. A thrill of recognition of what had just happened went through me, and I thanked Willum but also there was a feeling of peace washing all over me and my doubts and concerns were sloughed away.

Sometimes when I slept through the alarm, Willum used to whine and give little yowls until I got up.

After a cup of tea and a cigarette and constant thoughts of what had happened, I began to think that it was perhaps my imagination that had played tricks. By half past six, I was convinced it hadn't happened at all, just my imagination. Later on, when my mother came down, she said she'd heard what she thought was me 'crying or something', moments before I got up. 'Funny', she said, 'it sounded just like Willum, the way he used to call out to you'. So.......

On going to put batteries in the alarm clock, I found it was running as normal and it worked perfectly for the next four weeks before it did indeed need new ones.

Willum has been four more times since then, always when there is complete silence, no winds or anything; he could be clearly heard and not confused with any other noises. Always unexpected and when I'm thinking of something other than him, but no further interference with the alarm clock!

*****

# *(A different) Janet and the Fox.*

*Janet wrote -*

I had a very vivid 'dream', in which a fox cub came to me and I hand fed it. Two weeks later the dream came to life.

Half of my garden is fenced off for my West Highland White terrier and the other half is left open, so that any passing wildlife can visit in safety, (from my terrier that is!).

Two weeks after my 'dream', I was looking out from my conservatory window one day, when I saw a fox walking behind the wire fence of the fenced off area; just as the fox had in my dream.

I know a little about foxes through visiting the local animal sanctuary. On one occasion when I was there, the owner held a fox cub to my face and let me stroke it; so I wasn't at all afraid of the visitor to my garden.

The fox came back every day but one day in particular, I noticed it was holding up a hind leg, as though the leg was hurting, so I rang a nearby fox rescue centre for advice. They said the best thing would be to give five tablets of Homeopathic Arnica 30c - if I could get the fox to take it. I use Homeopathic remedies and had the tablets to hand but the only way I could think of, to get the tablets into the fox, was to make a sandwich of bread and honey, put the tablets inside it and offer it to the fox, exactly as I had in the dream.

As I held the sandwich out to the fox, I noticed that its eyes had a very soft expression. I spoke softly to it and said 'This is your medicine honey'. The fox opened its mouth, took the sandwich and swallowed it, just as it had in the dream. From that day on it was known as 'Honey'. The leg gradually got better and I enjoyed the fox's visits every day for a year, until sadly it was killed in a road accident.

Some while later I had pneumonia and was at a very low ebb. At times when I was feeling particularly low, I would walk outside, sometimes in nearby woods and always at some point, a fox would appear from nowhere, which always lifted my spirits and made me feel better. I feel that the fox is my special animal and that their appearances are meant to comfort me.

*Janet Continues;*

Gypsy was a black Miniature Poodle belonging to me and unfortunately he suffered from epileptic fits.

About half an hour before each fit happened, I would notice a smell of electricity and was able to get Gypsy to the vet's before he had a seizure. On one occasion the vet asked me how I knew when to bring him in and I told him it was because I could always smell electricity. He was very sceptical and asked what electricity smelt like. I described it as - like the smell you get when you first turn on an oven hotplate.

*****

I often walk in Ashdown Forest and always, in no time at all, I've got seven, (always seven), crows following me. I feed them on cheese and peanuts. Apparently, crows are believed to be incarnations of lost relatives or friends and on one occasion, a passing horse-rider actually called to me, 'I'm glad you're looking after your friends'!

*****

# Jennifer  -  Steffi and Denzil

**Jennifer wrote  -**

I have been an animal lover all my life and over the years have loved and lost five dogs, - two Cavalier Spaniels and three Bernese Mountain Dogs.  Some were old and very ill; others went young and the pain was heartbreaking.  Last summer my first cat died and I was distraught.

One of the hardest aspects for me is that, unless you are also an animal lover, it is impossible to appreciate the grief that accompanies such a loss.  Fortunately for me, my husband and parents also love animals and they have supported me on these occasions.

I think what I have learnt over the years, is that when it comes to our pets, we have to treasure every single day we have with them, for we never know when they'll be taken from us.

Two of my pets, a puppy and a cat, returned to me after they died.  I found it very painful to write about them, especially with my puppy, who died fourteen years ago.  I suppose through time I have put this to the back of my mind.

******

**Steffi (Forgeman Festival) 26 March 1991 – 16 August 1991**

I first encountered Bernese Mountain Dogs at a Championship Dog Show in 1987 when I was 17 years old.  I had owned dogs from the age of nine, (two Cavalier Spaniels) but was desperate for a large breed to show.  I fell in love with Bernese from the moment I saw them and contacted a breeder.  Six months later, when I was 18 years old, I got my first Bernese puppy.

I joined the Breed Clubs and decided to write a long letter to one of the most influential breeders in the UK at that time, pouring out my feelings for the breed and asking if they would put me on their waiting list.   Although they very rarely bred litters, to my amazement, they wrote back, saying that if they did ever breed a

litter, they would put my name on the top of the list and let me have
the pick.

I corresponded with them for three years, until in 1991, they bred
their first litter in seven years. One was a beautiful bitch puppy and
they said I could have her. We travelled to Redditch to collect her. I
was 21 years old – what a perfect 21st present!

I called her Steffi. She was adorable and I built up a fantastic
relationship with her. I had so many hopes for her; she had
wonderful lines but first and foremost she was a family pet, living in
the house as all my dogs have done. She was my pride and joy.

One Friday evening in August, when she was 19 weeks old, my
father took her and our other dogs out for a walk. He walked along a
footpath and let the three dogs off the lead. Just then, two boys on
bikes appeared. Steffi got a terrible fright and began to run. My dad
yelled at the boys to stop but, to his horror, they began chasing her.
She kept running until she was out of sight. My dad ran home and
told me what had happened. She was nowhere to be seen.

I put on my coat and instinctively ran to a busy road; a dual
carriageway, that runs behind my parents' house. I ran along the
central reservation and I could see her black body lying on the road.
Whoever had hit her hadn't even stopped.

When I got to her I tried to lift her. She was still warm but her
body was so heavy. I lay on the road beside her, hugging her body as
cars and lorries thundered past. Eventually a passing motorist helped
the two of us into her car and drove us home. When my parents
realised what had happened they were in a state of shock and I had to
be heavily sedated.

The days that followed were some of the lowest in my life.
Steffi's body lay in the garage, as I had decided I wanted her to be
cremated. She was taken away on the Monday, in a beautiful white
Mercedes. I honestly thought my heart would break.

Exactly a week after she died, at 8.40pm on a Friday evening, I
went out for a walk alone and picked some flowers. It was getting
dark and I walked down to the spot where her body had been. There
was still blood on the road. I lay the flowers down and began
praying for her and stood for a few moments, contemplating.

As I turned to go I gasped, for there was a large ginger cat, sitting at the side of the road watching me intently. I had never owned a cat and was a little afraid of them but this one put me instantly at ease. I couldn't believe that it was sitting so close to such a busy road with such heavy traffic. It didn't seem in the least afraid.

As I began to walk home it began to walk along beside me. I had never seen this cat before in my life and found it so strange the way it was watching me. When I reached home it followed me up the driveway. I didn't know what to do so I went indoors, closed the door and then looked out the window.

Suddenly it dawned on me, - was this Steffi coming back in another form? Behind the glass I whispered 'Steffi – is that you?' Suddenly the cat jumped onto the windowsill and sat staring at me intently. I whispered to it for a few seconds, before it jumped down and disappeared. I had never seen that cat before and it never appeared again.

Was it Steffi? I don't know but I know Steffi was behind this happening. Despite my grief, I gained huge comfort that she was letting me know she was alright.

*******

## Denzil  *(11 December 1995 – 9 August 2004)*

I'd never really been a cat person and having lost a young dog in tragic circumstances, had decided I didn't want any more pets, as the heartbreak was too much to bear. However, one day at work, a colleague told me her cat had unexpectedly given birth to three kittens. Two were large and healthy and already spoken for but she wasn't sure if the third, a tiny black one, would even survive.

I asked if I could go and see it after work, (just to look I told myself) but the inevitable happened  - I fell in love with him and asked if I could give him a home, if he survived.

I got him home at eight weeks old. He was hardly much bigger than a mouse, so I took time off work and hand fed him on milk and baby food. Everywhere I went he went. He would walk from room to room with me, chattering away. I lived alone at the time and the two of us became inseparable. He slept on my bed, sat watching TV on the couch with me and even when I was in the bath, he'd be perched on the edge, playing with the water.

When I began to let him outside I was afraid he'd start killing things, so I put a bell on his collar but he just sat on the windowsill, watching birds.

When I married and had my daughter, he never once showed any jealousy or resentment towards her.

Last summer we moved to a house with a large garden and I was so pleased that after so long in my flat, he now had a garden to prowl around. He seemed to sense that this was his domain and would lie on the patio, sunning himself.

He was eight years old by now and although I had noticed that he was sleeping more and eating less, I wasn't too concerned at first but then, within a few days, he started hiding himself away, wasn't eating anything and had stopped purring and chatting to me. I knew there was something very wrong and took him to my vet.

Even after many visits, the vet could find nothing wrong with him, so I asked for a scan. When the vet phoned me on my mobile I knew it was not going to be good news. He said the scan had revealed acute kidney failure – there was nothing that could be done and he would have to be given sleep. I asked, through tears, if I could come and be with him but the vet advised that it would be kinder to put him to sleep immediately as he was already sedated.

I felt so much guilt and grief that I'd been with him all his days but I couldn't be with him as he passed away and I felt angry that he'd been taken so suddenly; just like with Steffi, I didn't get to say goodbye.

My husband, daughter and I, all visited the surgery and held and kissed and cuddled him but I was so distraught that I had to run and leave. My husband undid his collar, with his bell and nametag and took it home.

We were all in such a state that night, especially me. I had difficulty getting to sleep but finally fell into a deep sleep. When my husband woke me the next morning he looked quite shocked. He told me he'd been watching Breakfast Television when suddenly from the kitchen, he heard the bell on Denzil's collar ringing. He looked round to see him, when it dawned on him that Denzil was no longer with us. He heard the bell again and walked into the kitchen. The collar and bell were on the worktop. My husband had never believed in such occurrences until this happened.

There was no explanation for this. None of our neighbours' cats wore collars and the sound was so clear. Later that morning, I heard the bell, again coming from the kitchen.

Over the next two days, I heard the familiar thud of him jumping down from furniture. I'd run upstairs thinking at first that a neighbours' cat had made its way into our house, then realised the house was empty.

One day I was lying in bed thinking about Denzil, very upset, when suddenly I felt him brushing against me, the way he always did when he came into bed beside me. It was incredibly comforting, knowing that my friend was still around.

*****

# Joan – & Lucky

*Joan lost her beloved Lucky, a tortoiseshell & white cat, at ten years old.*
*She wrote -*

I was heartbroken. They say hearts don't break, but they do. Mine broke but it is slowly mending now. Pixie, my new little bronze tortie kitten helps, also my lovely little dog Polo, who loved Lucky very much and is slowly coming to terms with a mad kitten who is determined to be her best friend.

The first two days after Lucky's death, I was inconsolable. I felt as though something was tearing my insides apart. I kept crying, 'God stop it hurting, I can't bear it!' Then I had a vivid dream.

Both my parents are dead, also my sister Jean, who died at 51 (and I miss her still). As Lucky died I kept telling her I loved her and that I was giving her to my sister. At important times I have had visits from my sister in my dreams (and I know these are 'astral' visits, not just random dreams), so I expected it to be Jean who first appeared in my dreams. But no, it was my dad, who died 35 years ago!

I was in a room I didn't recognise but it felt comfortable and there was my Lucky. She looked so well. Her lovely Tortie and white coat gleamed. I picked her up and hugged her and felt her soft silky fur. I put my hand on her tummy where that horrible tumour had disfigured her and her lovely fur had grown back smooth and silky, no tumour.

I turned round to a settee and there sat my dad, cuddly and comfortable wearing a grey sweater. I sat down next to him and said 'Oh, dad! It's my Lucky'. But when I looked at her again she had turned black. I said 'Dad, what has happened, she's turned black!' He said 'Don't you know, she can be any colour she likes here? She will change back for you, just watch.' Sure enough, she slowly turned, first to a bronze tortie and then back to her tortie and white.

I remembered then, that when one's astral body wanders about, one can wear what clothes one likes, or different hair colours.

After that dream the pain eased a lot. I knew she was with my family. I did have another dream where my sister appeared too and I had another cuddle with my Lucky. I know they will look after her.

Some people will say it was just dreams; wishful thinking but when one has had an especially close and loving relationship with an animal and they die, I'm sure they want to show us that they are still around and they want to ease our pain.

Through having Pixie, I've made a new friend, Rowena, who recently lost her favourite cat, Merlin. We have a lot in common and I feel as though I have known her for years. Rowena's mum died in 1987. She had always adored animals and had always had cats and dogs. The day before she died she had visited an old friend. She told this friend that she had always had a fear of death but the previous night she had had a dream.

In the dream, her parents appeared, together with her late husband and a large poodle that had been one of her best-loved dogs. They all greeted her affectionately and said ' We are ready for you now.'
She then told the friend that she was no longer afraid of death. She died the next day.

*****

**In a second letter, Joan had more news from Rowena -**

## Thelma and Robert

**Joan wrote** -

Rowena has a friend called Thelma, a super lady with several animals including a blue merle Border Collie called Robert. Everybody adores him. He loves cats. Thelma often looks after cats for friends, when they go on holiday. Robert lets them sleep with him and will put one of his front legs round them in a hug! Thelma is a great person. She is 71 but looks 50. She has been married twice, neither marriage worked but she eventually had a partner called Roy, who was a great guy and her soul mate. She had many years of joy with him but six years ago he died.

Thelma is a Wiccan and believes strongly that life goes on for our animals and ourselves. Shortly before Roy died, he saw Robert who was then a week old puppy and the runt of the litter. Roy fell for him, so Thelma asked if she could buy him. The breeder gave him to her free of charge.

Two years after Roy died, Thelma had a dream. She was walking down a lovely country road and there was Roy on the other side. He had a little dog on a lead. It was a brindle Whippet with a round white spot under his chin. Thelma ran across to them and said, 'Well it's about time you came to see me. How are you?'

Roy said,'Oh I'm fine now, I look after the dogs here. This one is called Spot.' Thelma joked about 'How original.' She woke up very happy.

She told her friend Jackie about her dream but Jackie, who is – or was – a sceptic, just said 'Yeah, yeah.' Some time later, Jackie asked Thelma if she would go to the dog rescue with her, to help her choose a dog. Of course they took Robert.

They looked and looked and Jackie just could not find 'her' dog. The lady who was showing them round asked them to wait, as she had to bring out a dog who was just being checked over. She came out with the dog and Robert's tail wagged. The dog was a brindle Whippet with a round white spot under his chin!* Jackie turned white and said 'Don't you say a word!' Of course, that was the dog she fell for.

*****

**\* Joan and Thelma think that he may be one of Spot's descendants.**

# Joanna – Jack, Magic & Stormy

***Joanna wrote to me. The following is taken from her letter -***

I have kept Whippets since 1990 and have had three instances of after death communication from adored dogs I have lost.

**Jack** was a very special dog. He came to me aged eight weeks and we had eleven great years together. In fact he changed the course of my life, as I am now a qualified animal homeopath and complementary therapist; a path I would never have gone down if I had not owned him.

Jack developed an auto-immune disease we believe to have been Systemic Lupus Erythematosus, with the added complications of chronically failing kidneys. He was seven years old at the onset of his very severe illness.

Against all odds he was brought back from the brink just in time. Whilst he had to take the steroid Prednisolone for the rest of his life, he had a remarkable quality of life, owed greatly I'm sure to the homeopathic remedies he was given, along with other complementary therapies. All these things were new to me at the time but I was so desperate to keep him going I was willing to try almost anything.

One day, about a week before Jack was put to sleep, he was lying in his bed in a strange way and I stood looking at him. I knew it was one of those days when he wasn't well but he wasn't really ill either. I suddenly realised that another of my Whippets, Stormy, was standing beside me, looking directly at Jack with what I can only describe as a 'gloomy face'. His head was lowered and his ears were flopped forwards. He held that stance for about two minutes, all the while staring at Jack, until eventually he literally shrugged his shoulders, gave a huge sigh and walked away, as if he knew there was no hope.

The loss of a treasured pet is always hard but when you have lived, slept and breathed an acute and life-threatening illness for four years, watching like a hawk for any slight symptom and doing your utmost 100% of the time, it is especially devastating.

Eventually of course Jack's kidney disease progressed to the point where we were in the dreaded downward spiral towards end stage kidney failure. This, with all its horrors, could not be allowed to happen, so on April 22nd 2003, he was put quietly to sleep in the back of my car.

My Whippets are exercised each day at our field and when they die, they are buried there, down by the Kingfisher river.

I took a friend and her 20year old daughter with me for moral support. We laid Jack to rest and very sadly made our way the 150yards back to the gate. As we reached it, my friend said (and still doesn't know why she said it, not being at all religious), 'God speed Jack, you're on your way now.'

At that moment I heard a noise and turning round we all saw the largest swan imaginable, flying low over the new grave. The sun was hot, a glorious April afternoon, akin to a summer's day. The most extraordinary thing was that as he flew over the freshly turned earth, he turned his head and looked back at us; a lengthy stare; before flying on towards Thame and the river. The sun glinting on his plumage turned it to silver.

We were rendered quite speechless by this sight as swans always fly very straight and direct. I have never seen one look back before.

My friend Liz gave me a sweet little posy of forget-me-nots and a card. She said the blue flowers reminded her of Jack; when she thought of him she saw forget-me-nots. A couple of weeks later, about seven o'clock one evening, I went onto the back lawn, feeling very down. Something on the newly mown turf caught my eye.

Lying on the grass, in full view, was a tiny and perfect sprig of forget-me-nots, about one and a half inches long. None grew in my garden, or those of my neighbours - where it came from, a complete mystery. I dried it and have it still, fixed to Jack's collar.

About the same time, he came back to me in a sleep-state dream. I was with him on some water meadows, not mine but at Wheatley, a village near Oxford, although we had never been there together in this life.

I was muffling him up in all his coats because he always felt the cold and wore several layers. It was as real as if we were in the light of day. I could touch his silky fur and he looked lovingly at me. When I woke I was broken-hearted because he was not with me but I have been comforted by the dream since. I think the words I wrote in memory of him say it all: 'Et in Arcadia ego' - 'And I am in Paradise.'

Two other of my departed Whippets have come back to me in sleep-state dreams.

**Magic** my first Whippet, a beautiful black dog, was put to sleep aged 12. He had severe spinal problems, chronic hepatitis and diabetes but again, had lived a full life, helped latterly by homeopathy and conventional medicine.

I was inconsolable. About two weeks later, he visited me in a sleep-state dream. We were at a dog show together. His coat gleamed like ebony. It was a wonderful sunny day and I was stroking him and admiring his sleek lines.

**Stormy** was a fawn Whippet that I lost through chronic kidney failure when he was eleven years old. Eight months after he was put to sleep, I dreamt that he came running into the kitchen where I live now, although he only had three weeks here before we had to say goodbye. He rushed to the water bowl and drank it all, something which had been happening in the last two weeks of his illness. He jumped against my legs and I could feel his heavy body, ice-cold.

My mother was here, which was strange as she lives about forty miles away and doesn't often visit. She is very elderly and uses a zimmer frame but in the dream she looked about sixty.

I said 'Oh no, Stormy's drunk all the water. He has kidney failure, he'll die.' Then I realised and said 'It's alright, he is dead'. Mother didn't answer and I woke up.

I have lost two other Whippets, neither of which has been back to visit yet but I now know that I will be re-united with all of them when I pass into light one day.

*****

# John and Lucky

### John sent an e-mail after reading 'OTRB' -

I lost my friend in 2001, just two weeks before his fourteenth birthday. His name was Lucky (Border x Spaniel). He was abandoned on a country hill, inside a bag. I was visiting some friends on a farm when he was found and brought in. I took him home with me and he turned out to be the best friend I would ever have. That was in 1988.

Over the years, he won hundreds of rosettes and trophies in the show ring and for obedience and agility, and also became a first class PAT (Pets As Therapy) dog.

He went everywhere with me; to have my hair cut, shopping, and to the pub; always riding in the front of the Land Rover in his harness.

The day he left was so very normal. We had been over the common playing and then to the pub for lunch. We arrived home and he had his dinner, but that evening he just left.

I was broken hearted. Something had gone inside of me and I felt completely alone.

In 2002, my wife and I went to a dog show at Victoria Country Park. We met a friend of ours who breeds Rough Collies and we were invited back to their camper van for a cup of tea. It was a warm day and my wife removed her coat and put it on the seat inside the camper van. At the end of the day, we arrived home and remembered the coat. I phoned my friend to arrange to collect it the following weekend.

We arrived at the house on the Saturday to collect the coat. They had a Tri-colour Rough Collie bitch that they had bred and which had been with them for seven years. To my amazement, she went out to the Land Rover, got into the front seat and refused to come out!

Both my friend and her husband tried in vain to get her out but failed and in the end, said that we had better take her home for the weekend. That was nearly two years ago and she has been with me ever since. Her name is Tanny. She plays on the same common and comes into the pub for lunch, just as Lucky did. She will do some of the things (but not all), that Lucky used to do.

To this day, we do not know why she left her home like that.

***John ended his e-mail by saying –***

I do hope with all my heart that the poem '*The Rainbow Bridge*' is true.

*****

# Judy  -  Great Danes

**Judy, (alias Joanne) and her Great Dane bitch, Lacey, appeared in 'OTRB'.  Judy rang me with an update, as follows -**

**1st. October 2004.**

'Lacey has now been back to see me several times.  On one occasion, I was sitting in the chair reading the dog paper.  I leant forward to lift my cup of tea from the table next to me and as I did, I felt pressure on my left shoulder.  Lacey had always had the habit of resting her head on my shoulder, so I was sure it was her and spoke to her, saying 'Mummy knows you're here.'

'A week or two later, I was in the kitchen and looked through the door into the dog-room.  Lacey's bed is still in there, with her ashes on the shelf above.  As I looked, I quite clearly saw Lacey's shadow on the bed for several seconds.  I went through into the dog-room and as before, acknowledged Lacey's presence by saying 'Mummy knows you're there.'

'My friend May had a Great Dane called Hamish.  He used to stay with me a lot and always slept on his beanbag in the kitchen.  May had nursed him for about three years with spinal problems but he eventually had to be put to sleep; that was just over a year ago.  Two or three weeks ago, I walked through to the dog-room from the lounge and as I did so, I looked into the kitchen and there was Hamish asleep on his beanbag.  I said ' Oh, you're a lovely boy Hamish.  Aunty Judy loves you.'

I was so excited I rang May to tell her that Hamish was back.

'Interestingly, Frank* and I have both noticed that we have moths indoors now; something that we didn't have in the past.  These moths don't flit about frantically round the lights, as moths usually do but seem quite calm and fly very slowly and gracefully.  They have only been apparent since Lacey died.

*****

*(Judy's husband)

# *Kayla and Molly*

### *Kayla wrote to me after reading 'OTRB' -*

In August 1987, I was driving to visit my sister, whose house, a short trip from my parents' home, was near a local golf course. I could see a dog wandering along ahead of me, at the side of the greens. As I got nearer, I could see it was a Greyhound and she was in an awful state. I stopped the car and went over to the dog, which looked at me and just sat down, exhausted.

So began my life with rescue Greyhounds and Lurchers. 'Honey' spent some time at the vets recovering, before coming to live with me. She was a beautiful fawn Greyhound, my 'Honey-bun'. Not wanting her to be an only dog, I rescued a five- month old brindle boy Lurcher, 'Tiger'. He was an innocent little chap, who despite being very poorly at first, later blossomed into my 37 kilo 'Handsome Boy'. Honey and Tiger became like mother and son.

I hadn't thought of having another dog, especially as Honey and Tiger were so close but I was told of a Lurcher bitch that had been living on the balcony of a flat in a particularly rough estate. The owner, the brother of an 'acquaintance', had lent the poor dog to his 'mates', for breeding, whenever his funds were low. She was only four years old but had already had two or three litters.

Although he was reluctant to give the dog up at first, the 'acquaintance' eventually managed to persuade him to, mainly because he was tired of clearing up the balcony when neighbours complained about the mess and smell.

The plan was that I would pick the dog up from the 'acquaintance's' house and take her to the 'waiting' kennel at the Celia Cross Greyhound Trust but when I saw her, I decided I couldn't put her through the trauma of kennels, so took her home. I've never seen a dog so frightened of humans.

I made up a bed for her in our small front room, with a gate across the door. She crept into the bed and stared wide-eyed at me, shaking. When I put her food in the room, she would wait until she thought I'd gone, creep out of her bed, pick up a mouthful and rush back to the bed to eat it, all the time watching the doorway. My heart went out to her. Goodness knows what she'd been through.

With much patience and long hours of just sitting in the room with her, she finally began to trust me. After three weeks, she eventually was brave enough to venture into the rest of the house with Honey and Tiger but the slightest noise would send her rushing back to her room.

As the weeks passed, she became increasingly fond of Tiger. He was such a happy laid-back lad that she felt confident if he was around. All through the summer, she became a 'normal' dog, playing with Tiger and chasing rabbits on our walks in the 'Happy Valley' in Coulsdon. Tiger and Molly, as I called her, became the best of friends.

Towards the end of the summer, Tiger, Molly and their friend Lofty the Greyhound, who often came to stay, all developed kennel cough. They were all put straight onto antibiotics and although both the boys made a speedy recovery, Molly just didn't improve. Despite a lot of drugs and care from my vet, she just seemed to fade and she passed away one Monday evening in late summer.

I was devastated. Six months just wasn't long enough for such a sweet dog to experience how life should be. I tried to console myself with the thought that at least she had had that time with us. She was cremated with the teddy that had helped her settle in when she first arrived.

I decided to scatter her ashes in the Happy Valley where she really had been so happy. On the side of the valley, I began releasing handfuls of ashes into the warm breeze. I watched as each one drifted down the valley before disappearing. The last handful moved towards Tiger.

Initially I panicked, thinking Tiger would get covered but once the 'cloud' had completely surrounded him, he lifted his head high, while the cloud remained motionless for several seconds, then wagged his tail and the cloud of ashes moved on once again down the valley.

I was overwhelmed by a knowing - that Molly was saying a final goodbye to her dearest friend.

I haven't told many people about this, I'm sure they'd think me mad but reading your book, I know now it was a final farewell.

It was two years later that I heard of another Lurcher, which had been thrown from a car. When I went to see her I knew there was something familiar about her. She was called 'Christie' by the kennel staff but it just didn't suit her.

Ten days or so later, when Christie had come home to us, mum and I were walking all the dogs together. It had been raining and we were trying to decide on a name that was more 'her', when suddenly, she squatted down and spent a penny in a puddle, just as Molly had always done!! She had so many characteristics of Molly's, that I am certain it was Molly returning for a 'proper' life. So, Christie became Molly 2! She and Tiger bonded immediately.

My beloved Molly (2), 'Bod', died on the 17th March 2005, aged 13 years, after finally having a 'proper' life.

\*\*\*\*\*

## Liz and Keady

*Liz is a friend of ours with Wolfhounds. She and her partner Jeff,*
*brought Mina, one of their bitches, over to Bailey. Liz bought a*
*copy of 'OTRB' while she was with us and some time afterwards, I*
*received a letter from her, which is included here with her*
*permission -*

Dear Wendy,

I sat down to have a look at your book last night and ended up
staying up all night until I finished it. I cried a lot whilst I read it and
for a long time afterwards, for you and Steve, for all the people who
shared their stories, but mostly for Keady.

I wanted to tell you about Keady when we were at your house but
even though she's been gone almost three years, I still can't talk
about her without crying, so I knew I wouldn't get through the story.

Keady was my first Wolfhound and I loved her with a passion.
She was the sweetest, gentlest and most beautiful creature I'd ever
met. She slept in my bed; she came everywhere I went, in all her life
we never spent a day apart.

When she became ill it was something and nothing at first. I knew
she wasn't her usual self but couldn't put a finger on it. I took her to
the vets, who convinced me she was fine, just a stomach bug,
antibiotics would sort it out.

This went on for about two weeks during which time I paid
three visits to the vets, always to be told, 'Don't worry, she'll be
fine.'

During this time she'd stopped coming on our daily walk to the
beach, then one morning as I was getting ready to take the other
dogs, there she was waiting by the car. My spirits lifted, I thought,
great, she must be feeling better, so off we went. The tide was in that
morning, so we walked along the cliff path that wanders up and down
through the sand dunes. If the dogs run ahead or behind, they
disappear from sight as they go in and out of the dips.

That morning, I had to keep waiting for Keady plodding along
behind. I kept turning back to wait for her to appear over the next
hill. We didn't walk very far and I sat for a while looking out over

the sea. Keady came to sit beside me while the others played around and as we sat there, I suddenly realised quite clearly, she hadn't come because she felt better, she'd come for one last walk and I knew in that moment she would never come again.

The next day she took a turn for the worse. I rushed her off to the vets where she collapsed in the waiting room. It turned out that she had a serious infection of the spleen. They decided they had to stabilize her before they operated, so I left her there to stay on a drip overnight. She died during the operation the next morning. I couldn't and never will forgive myself for letting her down, for leaving her and not being there when she died. My guilt and grief were overwhelming.

Jeff and I collected her from the vets and brought her home. It was a terrible day, pouring with rain and the wind howling as we dug a grave by the willow tree in our garden, (the dogs favourite spot), where we buried her.

The next day Jeff had to return to Brighton where he was working. It was just luck, (or coincidence), that he'd been home when she died.

In the days that followed I was hurting so much it was almost a physical pain and if it hadn't been for the other dogs I don't know how I would have got through that time.

Every night I went out to sit on the stones round Keady's grave, just to be near her. I'd hung a wind chime from one of the branches above. I'd heard that wind chimes ward off evil spirits. Whenever I was in the garden and heard the tinkling of the chime it was as though Keady was there.

Anyway, one night, desperate with grief, I took out my Tarot cards (I don't know how to read them properly, we'd just seen them in a shop and I liked them, so Jeff had bought them for me.) I shuffled the cards and asked my question. I just needed to know that Keady was okay and that there was something after this life.

The card I turned over was one called 'The Close' (death) and its divinatory meaning is – 'a time of change, the end of an emotional relationship and the beginning of a new phase. The inevitable transformation of all life, a change in the journey of the immortal soul'. In the Tarot, death is seen as a renewal of life.

That night, when I went out to the garden, there was a full moon just above Keady's grave and its light shining through the clouds looked like a silvery path that came down to just above the grave. It may have been just a trick of the light but I believe it was the sign I had asked for.

I never saw Keady but for a long time after she'd gone, whenever I took that walk through the sand dunes, I had a strong feeling she was following me and I kept stopping to look back, expecting her to appear over the hill, as she had on that last walk.

One more strange thing. When I first had Keady, we lived in Derbyshire and I had a friend, Penny, who I used to go out walking with. Penny had a little mongrel, Dinky, who was a rescue dog. Penny and I used to write occasionally after I moved to Wales but I hadn't heard from her for a while. When she wrote next, she apologised for the long silence, saying that she'd been through a very bad time. Her mother had died and on the 27th. September, Dinky, her little dog, had died from an infection of the spleen. It was the same date that Keady had died.

*****

Last year, as we were in the middle of moving to a larger house, Luke, Keady's life long mate, died quite suddenly and unexpectedly. We buried him beside her in the garden and although it broke my heart to lose my boy, it was a comfort to know that when we left, Keady wouldn't be alone because Luke would be with her. Just another coincidence?

And one more – Mina and Bailey's puppies were born on 27th September ('04).

# Lorraine and Merlin

### Lorraine wrote -

Merlin was a ginger and white kitten, about three months old, when my neighbour found him in the road a few years ago. We discovered his family didn't want him so I gave him a home. I already had two other cats, Wallace and Snowy. Merlin and Wallace got on exceptionally well. Merlin was a bundle of mischief, into everything, absolutely adorable. At night he would sit on my chest in bed and gently touch my face with his paw, then settle down on the duvet by my hip. He would also go out at night. He liked my undivided attention and, after I'd been reading a magazine in bed one night, the next day I discovered that he had ripped up all my other magazines that were at the end of the bed – all cat magazines!

Late one night, as I was going to bed, he went out. I didn't see him the next morning. I'd had a dream that I was hovering over a cat that was in the road dying. Later that afternoon a neighbour came to say there was a dead cat lying in a local alleyway. I knew it was Merlin. I went to see and sure enough, it was. I was heartbroken. He had blood coming from his mouth and when I spoke to my vet on the phone, he said it sounded as if he'd had either a traffic accident, or possibly a fall. My neighbour helped me bury him in the back garden.

I was devastated and so angry. He'd only reached eighteen months. I wanted to know where he'd gone. Why was post-death such a mystery? I spoke to a psychic, who said he was still with me and that I'd get another cat that was black and had been mistreated.
The week following Merlin's death, in bed at night, there was a warm patch in the place he used to sleep, so warm that I could feel the heat straight through the duvet.

For a few mornings after his death, a robin appeared in the garden. This was very unusual as there are normally only a few Blue-tits, no other birds. I read somewhere that the robin is supposed to represent the souls of the departed, come back to say thankyou.

As to the new black cat - a few weeks after losing Merlin a black feral cat suddenly appeared, at a place where I had previously rehomed a friendly feral cat with a friend. I thought he was very young (he's actually a runt) and he looked in need of care, so I gave him a home and called him Magic.

One other thing that happened was when I woke up early one morning to see a strong reflection of a white cat in my TV screen, (which was off). Shortly afterwards, my penpal wrote to tell me she had just had her white Persian put to sleep because of ill health.

*****

# Lynda and Oreo

**Lynda wrote after receiving a copy of 'OTRB' -**

In August 2003, I had to have my beautiful one year old, chocolate point Siamese, Oreo, put to rest. He had been diagnosed with FELV, and also, a tumour that sat close to his airway and meant he couldn't breathe properly. I could not even tell you in words how heart broken I was. I was totally devastated.

Oreo was very childlike; he was my shadow; my other half – my baby. To get up in the morning without him was painfully cruel. How I still miss him.

Three months after Oreo's passing, my family convinced me to get another Siamese but he had to be chocolate, I'd made up my mind about that!

I rang a few breeders but all kept saying the same thing. Either they didn't have any chocolate point, or ones that they had were spoken for.

I had one last breeder to ring, and then I was giving up. My mum said to me, 'Come on love, chin up, it will happen if it's meant to be.' So I rang the last breeder, and yes, she had a chocolate point boy available!

He had already been reserved for a couple in Birmingham but the gentleman had been involved in a road traffic accident, so they no longer wanted the kitten. I went to view him and boy, he was beautiful. I reserved him and six weeks later I fetched my new baby boy home.

I still very much missed Oreo, so, as a tribute to him, I gave my new boy a special name. Oreo was born in May, so I put the month of May into the middle of my new boy's name and came up with 'Omaya' – purr-fect!

I had only had Omaya a few months when he too fell ill. To my shock and horror, he was diagnosed with FELV. At the moment he doesn't have any tumours but is harbouring the feline leukaemia virus. My world shattered. I cried buckets. Many a time I've asked Oreo to watch over Omaya and to look after him. I often wondered if he could hear me.

One day, sitting in my kitchen with Omaya on my knee, having a love and a cuddle, my daughter took some photos of Omaya and me. When they had been developed, I was looking through them and I couldn't believe what I was seeing. Above my head on the left-hand side, it looks like my chocolate boy Siamese, Oreo. It looks as if he's sitting up begging. He is actually sitting the way I used to carry him around. His body would rest on my hip and his front legs would rest over my arm. You can clearly see the dark chocolate face and front legs. I am sure this is Oreo's way of letting me know he's watching over both Omaya and me. I take great comfort from knowing my boy is not far away and I'm sure when the time comes for Omaya to leave, Oreo will be there to greet him.

*****

*(See Photo page 76)*

# Mandy and Mommycat

*Mandy wrote -*

We caught 'Mommycat' in a humane trap in the back of a garden, after weeks of trying. Previously, we had managed to catch, neuter and re-home, all her offspring from the four years she had lived wild there. I can't remember exactly how many there were but they were all semi-feral and the numbers were multiplying at an alarming rate.

Eventually only Mommycat remained but we knew that if she wasn't neutered, the problem would just continue. Anyway, at last we received a call late at night, to say she was in the trap and so we went to collect her. She was wild and spitting and desperate to escape. As it was late we took her home and left her in the trap overnight in our dog room, with food and water, intending to take her to the vets for spaying the following day.

When we opened the dog room door the next morning, there in the trap, purring contentedly was Mommycat, complete with four brand new kittens - hence her name!

Well, to cut a long story short, Mommycat stayed with us for her whole life, though she never left the house again, despite having the option to. She never allowed us to stroke her but she would bunt around us when food was being offered. She lived with us for fourteen years, making her at least eighteen when she finally died.

After she went, because we were never close despite this long association, neither of us was unduly upset. We had other cats, who were affectionate and the dogs whom we adored and so Mommycat soon faded into our memories.

Some time later, maybe six months or so, I was coming out of the bathroom, thinking about what to cook for tea, when sitting on top of the stairs (in her usual place), was Mommycat. I saw her as clearly as if she were alive. She turned her head, looked at me disdainfully and disappeared!

When Phil arrived home, I recounted my unlikely tale and was astonished to hear, that my ever so sceptical husband, had also seen her on another occasion.

Mommycat then became a regular visitor. She always appeared around the landing, stairs and lower hall, exactly her territory in real life. She had lived in the spare bedroom and often I would find the indent of a cat-sized shape in the middle of the quilt.

We were not the only ones to witness these events. A lady came to buy a puppy and having used the bathroom, asked if the dogs got on with the cat. As we no longer had a (living) cat, we questioned her and she said that a long-haired, tabby and white cat had greeted her on the top of the stairs.

Another time, a carpet fitter was putting new carpet in the hallway. He too asked about our long-haired, tabby and white cat and commented on how fast she moved!

When we had a new front door fitted, the workmen came to find me, most concerned about the cat that had just run down the stairs and past them. They were worried about her crossing the main road but though they looked for her, they couldn't find her.

A friend came to stay and stopped in the front bedroom. In the morning, she told us that the cat had been playing with the zip on her overnight bag and had slept on the bed next to her. However, this morning she couldn't find her and she queried how the cat could leave the room when the door was shut. She physically blanched when we explained.

Mommycat continued to appear for many years. We even sometimes heard the familiar 'prurp prurp' noise she made. Our big bold Kerry Blue Terrier was petrified when she was about, running and cowering in the corner, whilst the half a dozen or so Mini-Wire Dachshunds never took any notice at all.

Last year we sold that house and moved about five miles away. Mommycat chose not to come with us, as we have had no sign of her whatsoever.

The only rather strange thing is, the day we moved in, a real live tabby and white cat came running to meet us. She moved in with us on that day and is here now. We have christened her 'Sallycat'.

*****

# Marguerite and Persian cat 'Oliver'

*Marguerite first wrote in February '05, after reading 'OTRB'. Six weeks previously she had lost her beloved Pewter Persian cat 'Oliver' and was finding it extremely hard to come to terms with his loss -*

We rescued Oliver nearly five years ago when he was seven years old, along with Amy, a tortie Persian, who was then three years old. When we first had 'Ollie', his tummy and back legs had been shaved as his coat was so matted and consequently, he was very difficult to groom. It took three years before he trusted me enough for me to groom him without having leather gloves on but eventually I could hold him upside down on my lap and he even let me comb his tummy. He would 'sit' like a dog and lick his mouth for a treat of ham and he followed us everywhere, patting us with his paw when he wanted attention or his dinner.

It was six o'clock on January 5th when I went to shut the cats in the front room, as the hairdresser had arrived. Ollie was walking just in front of me when he suddenly collapsed. I called out to my son and my partner, who were upstairs and they ran down but Ollie died about a minute later. We were all in terrible shock and I'm finding it difficult to come to terms with, even now.

We had a post-mortem done but the results were inconclusive and the vet said that, as his death was so sudden, the most likely cause was either a cardiac arrhythmia, or a brain embolism. My only consolation is that he would not have suffered.

I really hope that in the not too distant future, I will have some form of contact from Ollie to give me the evidence I am looking for.

*****

***This letter went on to say –***

Over twenty years ago, we had a Rough Collie dog called Kim. One evening, I went into the kitchen to make coffee and found her dead on the kitchen floor. She was eight and a half years old. The post-mortem revealed several tumours on her liver, which had ruptured into her stomach.

A week or so later, my daughter and I noticed a 'doggy' smell in the kitchen, as if Kim was still there.

At this same time, we also had Sophie - a dark tortoiseshell cat, Toby - a Pewter Persian and a tabby cat called Jenny, who lived to just over fifteen years. Eventually her kidneys failed and she had to be put to sleep. Some time afterwards, I had a strange dream in which I saw Jenny, very clearly, lying down, not on my lawn, as I would have expected but on my mother's. We were all standing round her, when I said 'She is dead' and then she suddenly got up and walked off. This 'dream' is still very clear in my mind, even now after over sixteen years.

In November 1999, I found a lump on Toby's side. The vet found that he had tumours in both kidneys and he only lived for just two more weeks, mainly on steroids.

About a month after he was put to sleep, my partner Graham was in the living room, when he heard loud clear miaows, coming from the area at the bottom of the stairs where Toby used to sit and miaow if he couldn't find us. I told Mark, my son, what Graham had said, thinking he would probably just dismiss it but instead, he said he'd also heard miaowing coming from the bottom of the stairs. I'm sure they couldn't both have imagined it!

One morning last year, I got up to go to the bathroom and as I walked across the landing, I heard a very clear miaow, just the same as Toby's. My other two cats at that time, Ollie and Amy, were shut in the kitchen overnight and anyway, neither had the same clear miaow as Toby had.

Five months after losing Toby, I lost Sophie. She lived to almost fifteen years and was put to sleep in April 2000, due to a tumour in her intestine. Some days after, I felt sure I heard the tapping of her claws on the kitchen floor but at the time, I thought I must have imagined it.

\*\*\*\*\*

***A further letter in April brought this news –***

I had another experience this morning while I was in the kitchen washing-up. I was on my own and looking out of the window when I heard a strange sort of miaow, sort of 'ma –a' and then once more. Without thinking, I said out loud, 'Just a minute Bear', (we call Amy 'Bear', because she walks like a little bear), but when I turned round, Amy wasn't there and then I remembered, she was upstairs asleep in our bedroom. Also, she has a loud, clear miaow, which she proved a couple of minutes later, when she walked into the kitchen.

I then realised it was Oliver's (Ollie) miaow. He always had a funny sort of miaow, never loud or clear. Ever since we lost him in January, I have kept thinking to myself, how I would really like some sort of 'evidence' to prove to me he is still around me and I guess that was it.

*(See photo page 73)*

# Another Marguerite  (Belgium)  and  Karma

*Marguerite e-mailed the following story from Belgium, of how her dog Karma saved her life and continues to watch over her from the other side  -*

May I go now?
Do you think the time is right?
May I say goodbye to pain filled days
and endless lonely nights?
I've lived my life and done my best
an example tried to be.
So can I take that step beyond and set my spirit free?
I didn't want to go at first,
I fought with all my might.
But something seems to draw me now to
a warm and living light.

I want to go, I really do. It 's difficult to stay.
But I will try as best I can to live just one more day.
To give you time to care for me
and share your love and fears.
I know you 're sad and afraid,
because I see your tears. I'll not be far.
I promise that, and hope you 'll always know
that my spirit will be close to you
wherever you may go.

Thank you so for loving me.
You know I love you too.
That's why it's hard to say goodbye
and end this life with you.
So hold me now just one more time
and let me hear you say,
because you care so much for me,
you'll let me go today.

I love you,
Your Forever Dog Karma.

Those words I read in the eyes of my beloved Shorthair Collie, Karma. All night I had stayed with him. He was so ill. With his head on my knees we talked. 'Do you remember all the wonderful things we did together, dear Karma?' The long walks in the forest. How you loved running around in the garden with Horry, your little friend? How you helped me to overcome the anorexia I had for 35 years? How we stayed at Daddies bedside, when he had to go over to the Light a few years ago? You knew then he would die and you tried to comfort me. How you helped me and urged me to eat more, to start fighting to get well again. I was extremely thin by then and nearly dying from starvation and now, now ... I looked in your eyes and saw your plea.

Luckje, my wonderful black and white cat was lying at your side and looked at me with big worried eyes. He seemed to say, 'Let Karma go to the Rainbow Bridge, please Mummy, he wants to go!' Luckje was your big friend.

Yes, I had to make the decision soon but also I felt that Karma hated to leave me. He felt my intense sadness. 'It's OK Mummy, I want to go', he said. 'Don't be sad. I promise you that I will send you another dog, so you won't have to walk alone. You will see, it's OK!' I wanted to say that I only wanted him, but instead I told him that he was free to go to that wonderful place, The Rainbow Bridge, where Fern, the Cardigan (Corgi) of Mummy's, who died two years ago would await him. 'And we will never really part, dear Karma. Love never dies! We will meet again!'

I was a very lucky child. Daddy was director of a farm of 1800 ha. At the age of four I was already allowed in our large garden, on condition that I took our yellow Labrador, Gem, with me. Well, we were inseparable, so that was no problem. My parents knew I was safe as long as Gem was with me. When I got older, I had all that wonderful space to walk, swim and play in, together with my animal friends. There were no children to play with but my animals were far better company. They taught me love and respect for all living beings and taught me the real values of life.

It was horrible when I had to leave them to go to school in town but I returned at the weekends and oh, how we were happy to be reunited. After I finished school I wanted to study to become a veterinary but Daddy, my hero and soulmate, got seriously ill. He had a few heart-attacks and of course I stayed home to look after him and my mother.

We moved to France and after living 25 years near Biarritz, we went to Belgium. We found a small paradise and I still live there. I love it. By that time, Daddy was very seriously ill. All his life he had been a great sportsman; an Olympic show jumper and he loved the outdoor life, like I do. So he had a strong body and although the doctors had told me 25 years before, that Daddy would not live much longer, thanks to the Lord he did. He had his black Labrador Beltza with him wherever he went. It was Beltza who kept him alive, he often said. And I believed him. They are now together and I am sure it was Daddy who came and fetched Beltza when he died a few weeks after Daddy was gone.

My parents loved all animals but mummy did not want me to have a cat but

that was my great wish from the age of 6 years old. I was allowed to have them outside and they lived happily with the sheep I had but I was not allowed to have them in the house. The last years of my fathers' life were extremely difficult. He could not accept his illness and there was so little I could do to make him feel better. I felt horrible about it and had to do something to keep going. I asked again if I could please have a cat but mummy refused. But I could have a dog, she said. She had her lovely Cardigan Corgis, Ferntje and Kirby, who I too loved dearly but I wanted a dog of my own. Because of my anorexia, I wanted to walk at least 4 hours a day, so it must be a dog who could follow. I decided to look for a Shorthair Collie, also a wish of mine from my youth. I found an address where puppies should be born in a few weeks time. There were five spoken for already. But I could get the sixth one if…..

Anxiously, I waited for the phone call. There were five pups born,

so no puppy for me. A few weeks later the breeder telephoned me, that he had heard of a poor four-year old Shorthair Collie, who lived in a dark barn. He was the beloved dog of a young couple but they divorced and the dog just stayed behind. 'Will you not give him a good home?' the breeder asked hesitantly. 'I have seen him and he is a sweet dog but also he is in a sorry state.'

Of course I said yes. To put a Shorthair Collie in a barn is a horrible thing to do. They are such sweet natured dogs. They love to be in a family and live only to please their people. They are also very sensitive dogs. He must be terribly hurt, being dumped like that. I loved him already.

Two days later, a woman brought him to us. When he came out of the car I could not believe my eyes. He could hardly walk and he was so thin and dirty but the most horrible thing was the total empty look in his eyes. He had given up. It took the woman exactly five minutes to unload the car and then she was gone.

Good riddance I thought. What a way to treat your dog.

My parents were shocked too and very glad that Karma, which was his name, was now safe with us. As soon as we were alone I washed him. Under his dirty grey/yellow colour a beautiful black and white coat was hidden but oh, how thin he was.

Next morning, I asked my vet to come and he found out that Karma had a very weak bowel, a sort of IBS and also he had an autoimmune problem. His nose had eczema that never really got better. The IBS we got under control with a special diet. Very slowly, with the right medicines and much love, Karma gained weight. He taught me the importance of eating good healthy food and for the first time since I had anorexia, I realised the importance of gaining weight.

When Karma got stronger, I started training him in obedience. He loved it but it took half a year before he really dared to start loving me. One morning, when we were walking in the garden, he suddenly jumped high in the air and started to run in small circles around me. He smiled and was so happy. I had tears in my eyes. Finally Karma dared to be happy again. He wanted to live; he was saved.

When Daddy and shortly afterwards Beltza had died, my mother

fell and broke her knee. She became totally immobile. I was very thin by that time and felt that I had to make a decision. I started eating now or I would join Daddy! That's what Daddy told me, one morning while I was walking in the garden. I clearly heard his voice.

"Do you really want to die, Marg? Do you want to leave mummy and Karma behind? Or are you gonna fight as I taught you to years ago? Don't let me down! Don't let them down! Go to a dietician today! Promise!'

It was then that I realized how far gone I was. I looked in the

# Mrs. Q. and Cindy

**Mrs. Q wrote** -

I have been privileged to receive confirmation that little ones of mine who have passed over, are happy. I have seen one, who was called Cindy, some six months after she passed over. I called my other dogs in late one evening, and seeing Cindy sitting in her favourite place on a low wall, called her also. My husband then reminded me that she had not been with us for six months and when I turned round again she had disappeared – but there was a lingering 'feeling' in the air and I knew that she was still with us in spirit.

I have also seen 'shades' of other dogs from the past, playing at the top of my garden, always just around sunset. This gives me a very happy feeling, to know that they are not lost.

*****

# Muriel and Laddie

***Laddie's story appeared in 'OTRB'. Muriel (alias Margaret) wrote again after reading the book, to add the following to his story -***

We lived in the middle of a terrace of houses and I became friendly with my next-door neighbour, who would have Laddie for the day when I went up to Surrey to visit my parents.

We never fixed a time for my return but the first time I left him, she said, he was fast asleep in the middle of the lounge, when he suddenly got up and sat on her sofa to look out of the window - I appeared a few minutes later. I thought at the time it was coincidence but it then happened every time I left him with her.

I do not drive, so it was not the sound of a familiar car engine and I never telephoned to say I was on my way.

\*\*\*\*\*

# Pam (America) & Majerle & Max

*Pam first e-mailed to order a copy of 'OTRB'. After receiving the book, she e-mailed with the following -*

When I ordered the book I had no idea that it was primarily about your Wolfhound, Sweep. I own Wolfhounds and have just recently lost my hearthound and very best friend, Marley. He was two months shy of his 11th birthday. On the night that I lost him, I had cried myself to sleep on the couch. When I woke up, the TV was on MTV (a station that I NEVER watch and the remote control was nowhere near me). They were just starting a Bob Marley special! That was his nemesis, although I spelled it Majerle. I just know it was my boy coming to tell me that he made it to the bridge and everything was OK. I can't tell you how much that helped me to cope with losing him.

Also, in 1999, I had lost my rescue hound Max, to osteo. I am certain he has come back to visit on two occasions that I know of. The first time was the day I picked up his ashes.

I had been looking for his St. Francis medal that I had misplaced for months. That day I had walked into a room that I had searched many times before and a light, (from a ceiling fan that hadn't worked since I moved into the house), came on and shone directly onto Max's medal, in such an obvious spot that a blind person could have found it!

The second time was when he made the stuffed bunny 'sing'. Max never really liked toys as he never had any extras as a puppy and was abused terribly. A few years after I got him he finally picked up a little stuffed bunny and found out that when you pressed his paw, it would play the 'Easter Bonnet' song. He would make the bunny 'sing' his song non-stop, until he finally wore out the microchip.

I had placed his favourite toy next to his ashes on the dresser. A year later, out of nowhere, in the middle of the night, the bunny started to 'sing' his song, just once. The next morning I gave the bunny's paw a press to see if maybe somehow it really had started to work again, but it was as quiet as it was for the two years after Max wore out the chip.

*Pam's next e-mail had the following to say -*

The first night I got the book I really only had time to give it a quick scan, and upon reading it more closely, I found it a very intriguing coincidence *(!)* that the date that I lost Marley was also February 27th. *(The date we lost Sweep.)* It's as if he guided me to this book for a reason.

# *Pat and Perri*

### *Pat wrote after reading 'OTRB'  -*

I have Cavalier King Charles Spaniels and have had them for the past thirty odd years.  At the moment I have three  -  two nine and a half year olds and a two year old, Harry, who I show.  Three years ago I lost my darling Perri, very suddenly at the age of three.  He had a fit, in fact three (fits) and was gone from us within twelve hours.

I was very interested in what you said about butterflies, as I remember in the weeks following Perri's death, I would sit out the back and at different times, a butterfly landed on my shoulder.  I didn't think anything of it till I read your book.  None of the dogs I have lost over the years have come to visit me; I wish they would.  Perhaps this was a sign from Perri.  I'd like to think so.

*****

## Peggy(Margaret) and Carl

*Peggy (Margaret – but always known as Peggy) is a friend of Janet with the Irish Wolfhounds, Gersha, Mahoney, Bevis, Jacob and Willum . Janet persuaded Peggy to write to me with the following experience -*

Eleven years ago, we lost Carl, our Pyrenean Mountain Dog. He was just two weeks off his eighth birthday. He was bought as a puppy from Lockerbie in Scotland and my husband said we should call him Locky but I remembered that we had passed Carlisle on the way and said it would be nicer to call him Carl, so that became his name.

Over the years we had many holidays together in our touring caravan. Carl's favourite place was the Shropshire Union Canal. He became a familiar sight there and the people on the boats used to wave to him and call his name, as my husband and I walked him along the towpath. After his death, I found it extremely hard to go back to this, his favourite holiday place and it was a long time before we did venture back there.

Eventually we steeled ourselves and returned to the familiar campsite near to the canal. One evening, sitting in the caravan after our meal and looking out of the window, we suddenly saw in the clouds, a perfect image of Carl's head. His ears, eyes, nose and mouth were clearly distinguishable and I can only describe it as a 'happy face'.

Over the years we saw that familiar 'happy face' many times in cloud formation, most often at the Shropshire Union Canal but occasionally at other holiday places we'd all been to. Not only did we find it a comfort but as time passed, we were able to replace the heartache of losing Carl with memories of the happy times we'd shared with him.

*****

# Polly - Our Dog-sitter

*We were away in Ireland and Polly was dog-sitting for us. One morning she had an unexpected extra dog!*

*Polly explains -*

11am. 19th August 2004

I'd had my breakfast and was taking my plate through to the kitchen. I'd been sitting in Steve's chair, (in the lounge), so had to pass the window overlooking the patio and garden to do so. As I passed the window, I looked and saw a dog lying on the patio, near the railings and carried on to the kitchen. As I put the plate down I stopped dead. I hadn't got any dogs out! I went back to look and it had gone.

I re-traced my steps to see if I could have picked up any of the dogs that were in their runs, in my peripheral vision. No. I checked this a couple of times to make sure.

I spoke to Steve on the phone. He said Sweep used to lie with his back to the railings, just where I had seen 'my dog'. I'm waiting for him to get back to show me exactly where – I know it will be the same place. *

What I can't make out yet, is why Sweep showed himself here and not with Steve in Ireland. Maybe he was checking me out for Steve!

\*\*\*\*\*

\* *(It was! – Wendy)*

# Sarah and George  - Jasper, Heidi & Monty

### Sarah wrote to me -

Jasper was a sable and white Rough Collie that my husband George and I bought in 1990.

It was obvious from the start that he was different to other dogs we had owned. As a puppy, he was precocious, domineering, wilful and a little wild. We had lots of advice about how to tame him but the only thing that worked was lots of love and he certainly got that.

With time, Jasper grew into a very loving dog, (although still keeping all the above traits) and a deep telepathic bond seemed to grow between the three of us. He loved our daughters, who were then teenagers but George and I were his, totally.

We had many happy years with him, although not enough. As he lay dying in the kitchen when he was 12 and a half years old, I raced home from work and when I walked into the kitchen, he lifted his head and swished his tail, as if he had been waiting for me. The vet arrived with a nurse and I told Jasper he could go now and that we would always love him. It broke our hearts and we decided to have his ashes brought home.

A few days later, we had a phone call from our vet, to tell us the ashes were ready for collection. We picked them up that night. That was when we realized that Jasper was still around.

That night, as I lay in bed, the instant I closed my eyes, I felt a rush of energy, just like a very strong wind and at the same time, I felt a weight on my stomach. I immediately said, 'Jasper' and I saw the most vivid picture of a young sable Rough Collie, aged about 18 months old – most definitely a young Jasper. The only way I can describe the feeling I got from this was 'ecstatic'. I told my husband immediately and he said he wished he could see him.

From then on I could smell him every morning as I walked into the lounge with my tea and toast – he always used to join me for this, pushing in front of me to get there first. The smell was very strong and was most definitely his smell in old age.

Just before Christmas 2002 (Jasper died in the July), I walked in from work, took hold of the vacuum cleaner and started the ritual of vacuuming the hall, as I always did before going on to the lounge. Suddenly I stopped and turned the cleaner off, as I could hear the musical/animated Mickey Mouse ice rink (a Christmas decoration) playing a tune. I walked over to the ice rink and could not believe what I was seeing. The figures were all skating on the ice, then suddenly, the music stopped but the figures continued to go round until they stopped too. I instinctively knew this was Jasper's presence again.

On a number of occasions after that, George and I saw a light like a round spotlight, near George's chair, when the room was dark.

Another day, after a long day at work, George was upstairs changing and shouted down to ask if Heidi (Jasper's daughter – a sable and white Rough Collie), was with me. I shouted back to say that she was and asked him why. He came downstairs and said he had just seen a sable and white Rough Collie next to him, which had then vanished.

A few weeks later, again whilst changing after work, George was just about to sit down on a chair which we have on the landing, when he felt a prod in his back. Jasper used to do this with his paw when he wanted feeding.

Then there were the times when the upper door of the Grandfather clock was open, even though we always kept it closed. We would close it and then it would be found open again.

I began to see Jasper frequently – and still do. I can only describe it as, when I close my eyes before going to sleep, a small light which opens up into a picture and I see Jasper running in meadows and frolicking, as he was when he was young, instead of being crippled with Arthritis.

One night, I hadn't seen him for a while and as I passed his photo in the bedroom, I kissed it and asked him if he had fallen out with me, as I hadn't seen him for some time. That very night, before sleeping, I heard his happy growling sound he used to make and saw such a vivid picture of him, almost as if he had come to order.

Shortly after Jasper's death, we were visiting some friends of ours who are Mediums. I took Jasper's lead with me and told them what had been happening. The one told me that Jasper was sitting next to me on the sofa and he apologised for making a hole in the hall carpet (which he had done over the years, by the Collie bed-making process!).  She said that he would wait for George and me and he would be the first person we would see on passing and she said, he emphasized the word 'person'.  We smiled, as we always said to one another, that we expected him to step out of his dog-suit and tell us he was really human.

These particular friends live many miles away from us and did not really know him, or his traits; only that we loved him.  We took this as evidence that it was Jasper.

Since his death, his daughter Heidi has changed from the quiet bitch she was and picked up a lot of his traits, e.g. singing when I sing, crying with jealousy if George and I touch or kiss and many more funny little things he used to do but she didn't.

Over the last twelve months, we lost Jasper's old sparring partner, Monty, a black and tan, Cavalier King Charles Spaniel, aged 14 and a half years.  A few weeks ago (March 2006), when I saw Jasper just before falling asleep, I saw him playing with a small dark animal but I couldn't hold the picture.  However, if somebody put a gun to my head, I would say it was Monty, - they were chasing round and playing as they used to in this life.

As far as George and I are concerned, this is all the evidence we needed, that Jasper is still alive and happy 'over the Rainbow Bridge' with his friend, and waiting for George and I.

*****

# Shirley, Kev and Jud

**Shirley wrote -**

Thankyou for sending the book – I couldn't put it down. I'm glad that I read it because I know now that other people out there in the big world have had the same sort of experiences that we have. I'm drawing comfort from this and I'd like to tell you about what we have experienced.

Jud was our first rescued (Irish Wolfhound) hound. He was five years old when we had him and one of the big boys height-wise, an absolute gentle giant. He settled in well and got on great with our other hound, Blue. He was a typical Wolfhound, sharing his settee with me and posing in front of the camera.

Came the dreaded day in February 2004, he passed away with heart trouble. He was 8 and a half years old and a fighter to the very end. We had three and a half glorious years with him – he was one of the family. When Jud didn't come home from the vet's with us, we were devastated. When we left the vet's, we went for a short walk to get some fresh air and then started our journey home. Robbie Williams' 'Angels', was playing on our local radio station at the time. Every time I hear that song I think of Jud. We arrived home and fed our other dog Blue. She was waiting for Jud to run into the house and go straight to his bowls – but he didn't. Blue was looking for him.

It was a horrible experience.

We felt guilty. Had we done the right thing? We felt awful; distressed. It was hard to come to terms with it - no Jud. Basically we were a mess emotionally for some time. The three of us stayed downstairs that first night. Nobody slept, we were thinking of Jud.

Jud ruled the settee, it was his - you could share from time to time! The next day, we could see him stretched out on it - siesta time. It was reassuring and in another way, upsetting. He appeared for a few seconds and then he was gone. This happened every day until in the end we had to change the suite because we found it too upsetting at the time. We don't see him on the new settee – no more visual contact.

It's been over a year now.

We sense his presence from time to time. You have the feeling that you are not alone. My husband Kev and I, have both had the same shared experiences. Jud appears from time to time – we feel his presence. We live opposite the woods and when we look out of the window we both feel a nudge, (separate times), on the top of our legs. It's Jud, wanting us to rub his ears and his head; he wants a cuddle and a chat. We both feel ourselves doing this and then you look down and he's not there.

I have felt his presence first thing in the morning when I'm getting ready to take Blue out for her first walk. I get a hefty nudge on the bum – just to hurry me up. I manage to stop myself banging my head against the door or wall and then I can hear myself saying 'OK. OK, I'm doing my best; there, I'm ready, let's go.' Then I realise I'm only taking Blue out. That has happened numerous times.

Also, at breakfast times, we all, including Blue dog, stare at the patio doors. We know Jud is there, watching us and slobbering, wanting his piece of toast.

After reading your book it was a great relief to know that, out there, other people have these experiences and are willing to share them. We both thought that we were seeing or imagining things; even going mad! Now we feel normal.

We can understand now. Also, we know now by her actions that Blue can feel his presence, or even see him. She never used to do these things. It's reassuring that Jud comes home from time to time and is keeping an eye on us. Wherever he is he's happy.

*****

*(See photo page 77)*

# Su, Bramble and Oscar

*Su's (alias Jenny) story of Bramble and Oscar was included in 'OTRB'. After reading the book, Su wrote again to add the following about Oscar-*

I thought you might like to know that I have had one more visit from Oscar. Once again, this took the form of a very clear dream. He was smiling up at me in his mischievous way and then got on this sledge and took off on the snow. This is probably not as bizarre as it may seem at first, as he would always try to slide a paw over frozen water when it was icy. Anyway, I think this means that he is having a wonderful time. When we first lost Oscar, I used to worry if he was alright. He was often in trouble in this life, getting lost, or pinching food, - his main hobby! I used to wonder what he was up to, so perhaps he was just letting me know.

I was interested in Ray Gildea's comment, ('OTRB'), that humans can return in animal life form for earthly experience. I do not like to anthropomorphize but we always said, that Oscar thought he was human. His body language, facial expressions and reasoning, were all totally human. It was so easy to put words into his mouth – we all did it. I wonder if this could account for his interest in human type activities? Anyway, I hope to find Oscar again when my time comes.

Thinking back to the years when we only had one dog, (we have been a multiple dog household for the past ten years), I always felt guilty when we got a new dog after losing an old one, as though I was betraying their memory. I remember that I had a few dreams where Henry, our old Springer Spaniel, appeared along with the dog/s we had at the time of the dream. I always had the feeling that he was really very old but had somehow come back to us.

*****

## Jill and Larry

***Jill (alias Sheila) sent in Larry's story for 'OTRB' and wrote again
with some incidents of telepathy relating to her dogs -***

We had two friends who owned Shelties, some of which were our
breeding. In both cases, I always knew when it was either of them if
the phone rang. When I rang them, their Shelties would rush to the
phone and stand by it wagging their tails furiously – something they
never did at any other time.

After my husband, Graham, died, my daughter used to ring me
every Monday morning at 8.45. The dogs would go and stand by the
phone a few minutes before it rang. My daughter died very suddenly
six years ago. It was several weeks before the dogs stopped waiting
by the phone.

*****

# Terri and Lucy

### Terri wrote to me about Lucy, her beautiful white cat -

Lucy came to live with me permanently in 1998. I travelled to Chester on Boxing Day, to bring her back to her new home, having met her two years previously. I could see then, that she was a very unhappy girl, as she was in a hostile, noisy environment. So when her owners decided they didn't want her, I couldn't wait.

A journey that would normally have taken three hours, took six to seven hours. We travelled through horrendous weather, with Lucy answering me as I talked to her constantly.

Back home, it was to take quite a few months before she realized that I meant her no harm. I adored her.

She was independent on her walkabouts. In the evenings, after showering, I would settle to watch TV and she would charge through the house, jump into my arms, feet tucked under, so her head was nestling under my chin or neck and there she would stay until it was time for bed. She would charge up the stairs and wait on the bed until I was settled. Then she would lie on her side, with her head on the pillow facing me; I could feel her breath on my forehead. If I was restless, she would curl around the top of my head. We became soulmates and I could not imagine life without her.

But, then came the horrid day, when she was killed in the lane outside the house. I was absolutely distraught. I picked her up and lost all reason. For me, the world had ended.

Nothing made any sense anymore. The house was dead without her charging around and chattering.

Tim, our vet, brought her ashes home and they were placed in a glass corner cabinet with a forget-me-not flower on the casket.

That same night, I felt a light movement on the bed, then felt something walking up the side of me. It came up onto the pillow and with it, a smell of flowers, like carnations, (Lucy's favourite flowers.) I said 'Is that you Lucy?' Then I felt a soft breath on my face.

Since that night, I have seen Lucy walk through the lounge, where we had our nightly cuddles and have also seen her by her chair. I've felt her around my ankles and seen her walk through the kitchen, passing me, to go into the lounge, to get onto her side of the settee. I've also felt a light pressure resting against my thigh when I've been sitting there.

I think it must be somehow significant, that she died at the eleventh hour on the eleventh day of her eleventh year. Although I only had her for two years, she was unique and I miss her terribly. I look forward to the time when we meet again.

*****

# Tracey and Penny

**Tracey has a Wolfhound puppy, Myrtal, sired by our stud dog, Bailey.**

**She e-mailed the following -**

Had a butterfly incident the other day whilst walking Myrtal in the park. Was watching where I was going on the grass, because it had been raining very heavily and the river had burst its bank in one part of the park. Whilst I was looking down on the ground to avoid the muddy puddle, there was a Red Admiral butterfly just within stepping distance! It flew right up as if it was going to fly into my face and when I stopped dead in my tracks, it was nowhere to be seen! I would like to think that it was a message from my old Weimaraner, Penny, because it was the third anniversary of her death and she had been in my thoughts a lot. I think that she was giving Myrtal the OK!

\*\*\*\*\*

# Vanessa - Feathers

*Extract from E-mail from Vanessa, (alias Debra), whose photographs of spirit dogs, Hunter and Fidget, appeared in 'OTRB' -*

I am taking the book with me tonight before we start our paranormal investigation, so the other members can have a look too. A group member, Lisa, lost her Siamese cat on holiday a few weeks ago. She went missing and I don't know if you believe in Angels but I prayed for her cats safe return every night for four nights and each morning I found a white feather in my house. On the 5th day, I found another white feather and a text message from Lisa saying that the cat had come back safe.

*****

# Willeke  (United States) & Olaf

*Willeke now lives in the Netherlands but was living in the USA when she first e-mailed to order a copy of 'OTRB'.  The following was included in her first e-mail  -*

I lost my precious Wolfhound 'Olaf', in March last year, quite unexpected and have been hoping to 'see' him but nothing has happened.  We buried him in 'his' garden but were in the middle of our move from Ireland to America, so I'm afraid the distance is just too big, if that's at all possible.

I have experienced other extraordinary 'sights' but not since he died.  It was when he was in quarantine in the State Facility in Dublin and was supposed to be moved to private quarantine in Kerry at the end of a specific week, but earlier in the week I suddenly 'saw' him running through green fields.  In the evening the phone went and it was the lady of the private quarantine who said, 'Guess what?' and I said, 'They let them go a few days early?' and she was flabbergasted that I knew.

I'm just telling you this so you know that I really know there is more between Heaven and earth!

*In her next e-mail, she sent a lovely picture of Olaf and had the following to say  -*

I should have known that distance doesn't make a difference, for I had one other experience, where the distance was even larger.  It was when I lived in Australia.  I had had to rehome my two Wolfhounds, Hazel and Cormick, because of the distance between the Netherlands and Australia and the quarantine but when I had been in Australia for a few years, while I was milking cows, I suddenly saw a flash of Hazel (she appeared in the fountain that we had behind the cow yard, in a swamp, of all places).  I later calculated that must have been around the time that she died.

*After I'd sent the book to Willeke it was a while before I heard from her again. When she eventually e-mailed it was to say -*

It's been a while after I got your book and I read it right away.

I sort of 'talked' to Olaf, after reading the 'Rainbow' book and told him how sorry I was about the way things had been and hoped that he would forgive me and that I would so much like to get a 'sign' from him. A few days later I woke up one morning with him howling next to my bed – at least that's how it sounded! I jumped out of bed to check on the dogs and then I realized that this was Olaf's specific howl when we came home, - not one of my current dogs makes that sound. I felt that this was his way to let me know that he understood and that all was well.

*****

*(See photo page 80)*

# Susan and Chuchu

**Susan wrote -**

## June 2006

Last week we lost our elderly Siamese boy and for the first time in my life I do not have a cat. We loved and miss him very much and I thought I would like to let you know of something rather strange that has happened.

Looking through the film reviews in the Radio Times shortly after his death, I saw that the musical 'The King and I' was to be shown on television this week. We had chosen the name of the King's eldest son, Prince Chulalongkorn, for our Siamese boy, when we had him as a kitten nearly fourteen years ago. It could be coincidence but even if he did not actually arrange the scheduling of this film, I am sure that our Chuchu, (as he was usually known), drew my attention to it, so that we would know he was still there.

Something similar happened when our Scottish Terrier, James, died many years ago.

We were watching a motor racing broadcast, when the camera switched away from the track and focussed for several seconds on a Scottie, sitting all alone on a small table at the edge of the crowd of spectators.

One of our Irish Wolfhounds, who weighed over twelve stones, could tiptoe silently into the kitchen if he thought he could purloin something tasty – and although he died ten years ago, to this day I can still sometimes sense his presence when I am preparing food. Once or twice, shortly after his death, I caught a fleeting glimpse of his long grey legs as I turned away from the larder.

I don't pretend to understand it but I am sure they are all waiting for us somewhere.

\*\*\*\*\*

# Amanda  -  Tia

*Amanda wrote, after reading 'OTRB', with this amazing story of how her dog Tia saved her life and an account of Tia's many visits since crossing over -*

It was a humungous comfort reading your book and learning of other people who have had similar experiences.

I used to own a Rottweiler bitch called Tia, (Ritonshay Royal Ocelot - 28th July 1992 - 18th August 2004), who regularly gave demonstrations showing what an extraordinary and talented dog she was, also TV acting appearances. She was a real-life "Lassie" with the things she could perform!

The most heart-warming moment of all came from a little Rainbow (pre – Brownie) Guide's home-time prayer, after Tia had visited and given them a demonstration.  She prayed "Thank you, God, for Tia".

Tia was a Television & Film Dog and Rottweiler Personality of the Year (The Kirt Memorial Cup) 1999, 2000, 2001 & 2004.  She was shortlisted for the Golden Bonio Awards, 2003 and was Daily Mail Dog of the Year, Gold Medallist award, 2004.

Although she was my first Rottweiler, she was not my first dog. She was just seven weeks old when I got her and a present from my ex-boyfriend. She was a tiny, black-and-tan, ball of fluff, resembling a little bear cub - especially from behind when she walked, or tried to run.  Back then I wasn't to know what an exceptional dog Tia was going to grow up to be. She was one of life's extra-special dogs, and truly, a once-in-a-lifetime dog.

By far the smartest and most tear-jerking thing Tia ever did, was three months before I had to have her euthanased, when she saved my life.

On Saturday 15th May 2004, in the early hours of the morning, whilst away on a house-sitting job, I was laid on my back asleep, in the bottom half of a child's bunk bed, with Tia asleep by the side of the bed. I suddenly became aware that I was desperately trying to gasp for air, completely unable to breathe in or out, open my eyes or move my body. My lungs felt very painful, as though they were about to burst. I was only able to turn my head desperately from side to side, in an attempt to free the obstruction that was blocking my airway, but to no avail.

Suddenly it was as though my head had lifted from the pillow a few inches, and I was staring at my body from the chest down, lying there motionless under the duvet as though paralysed. My head then went back towards the pillow, and as it did I went into the kind of darkness you see when your eyes are shut. Following this, I immediately went on to experience the most indescribable sensation.

I started to fall away from my body, dropping out of it through my upper back (between my shoulders). I fearfully knew I was completely out of control of what was happening to me; I was separating from my body.

Panicking about falling into the vast emptiness below me, I very quickly said "I don't want to be doing this, I'm going to fall", in the vain hope that somebody would hear me and stop what was happening to me but nothing or no-one was taking any notice of me. I continued to come away from my body, and parted from it completely. I was surprised and shocked that I hadn't fallen and plummeted into nothingness on leaving my body but instead, very gently and very slowly, I was floating down away from my body. I was becoming completely at ease; the further I drifted away, the less I became aware of my gasping for air. I wondered, as I was floating down, where I was going to end up but I didn't care; I was now feeling so peaceful and totally relaxed as I slowly drifted further and further away from my body.

I continued to float very gently down in the darkness, still unable to see anything, when suddenly, high up above me and to my right, so very far, far away in the distance, I could just hear Tia barking. Instantly, the tone of her bark hit me; it was a tone of bark I'd never heard her use before, so very soft and gentle. I could not see her, only hear her.

On hearing her barking, my whole body's immediate reaction was, "I've got to get to Tia". Instantly, I stopped gently floating down, and started to journey back up, still out of control and a passenger. All the time I was rising, my whole body felt that I urgently needed to get back to Tia. All I kept thinking was "I've got to get to Tia", but I was only travelling back up at twice the speed I had been floating down. I still had no control over what was happening to me, so I had to be patient and accept it.

As I approached re-entering my body, I anticipated that the same sensation I had felt when I separated from it, (indescribable but not unpleasant), would happen again. It did! Completely inside myself again, I immediately sat up in bed, pushing the duvet that had been suffocating me, free from my face. I reached down to make contact with Tia, to gently rest my hand on her side, as I always did when I wanted to let her know that everything was OK.

Following this, Tia's behaviour was very strange and unusual. Her ears were erect and her eyes were like saucers. She stared at me very intensely, straight into my eyes and held this penetrating stare, not moving a muscle. Looking hard and deep into me, I could feel she was telling me, "You're out of danger now". She held this intense stare for a few moments longer, then lay flat out on her side and went to sleep as though nothing had happened, apparently knowing I was now safely out of danger.

Apart from having a head which literally felt like a squashed tomato for about an hour afterwards, (through suffering from lack of oxygen), the tearful shock of what Tia had done for me didn't hit home until the next morning. She had given me the ultimate gift a dog can give to its owner. She had saved my life. It is the most immensely precious, weird and tender feeling, knowing you owe your life to your dog - a completely different species.

I know, had Tia not been with me, to call me back from the out-of-body experience I was having, I would not be here today to tell you this story but instead, would have suffocated in my sleep.

Tia had saved my life. It was a huge shock in itself realising just how very close to dying I was. In the traumatic three months that followed I had to watch "my girl" - the dog that saved my life, slowly deteriorate and then, finally, I had to arrange the day to end her life. She had saved my life and I had to decide when to end hers. She went with dignity, at home. I would not allow her to suffer.

*****

I wish I'd kept a note of the dates and times of all the ADC's and weird things happening but I didn't. I didn't expect them to keep happening and never talked about them much. I only tested the water with a few close people; you can see the disbelief in most people's faces. It is a great relief to be able to talk about it freely now, without being thought insane and hallucinating!

\*\*\*\*\*

It has been nearly two years since Tia's death (18th August 2004), and I still get the odd visit from her every now and again. I find these visits very upsetting emotionally, as they remind me strongly of my loss but, at the same time, they are extremely comforting. I wish we could be in contact every day.

The bond between Tia and myself was so incredibly special and close it was magical. We were 'inside each others' heads'.

As an example; one evening Tia 'called' me home from approximately six or seven miles away. The vibes I was getting from her were just too strong to ignore. So I turned my car round in the middle of Henley, forfeiting my pre-paid Pilates class to return home, thinking as I did, "I'm coming home, Tia." On the way back, very uncertain of my actions, I thought to myself "I've lost £10 on the Pilates class and everything will be O.K. when I get home." To my surprise, on my return, I found Tia panting, upset and dribbling, waiting for me just behind the front door. My relief was immense that I had come home.

Judging by the saliva spots on the carpet, she had been waiting behind the door for my return, for a good ten minutes or so, which is roughly the time it would have taken me to get back home. Within half an hour of my return, she was completely relaxed and flat out asleep on her bed.

This happened about three days after Bonfire Night, so I would guess that someone had upset her by letting off some late fireworks in the village.

\*\*\*\*\*

Going back to when the ADC's started....

I had had Tia euthanased at home and the vet had just left. In tears, I went upstairs and looked out of my bedroom window at the lawn, where yesterday Tia and I played with the Frisbee. I had been gently rolling it to her along the ground, so she could catch it in her mouth, without having to run after it.

I looked beyond the garden and up to the sky. There was the most beautiful double rainbow. The end looked very close to our garden; just a little way away. It was a tweak of a comfort; as much of a comfort as it could be. Just then, I felt it had come down to collect my precious Tia. This was the first of many little unusual 'happenings' that were to follow.

The next day, my friend drove me to the Cambridge Pet Crematorium with Tia's body. I needed to wait while she was cremated and bring her ashes home straight away that day. I could not bear to leave her there, so after saying goodbye, (or what I thought was to be goodbye), in the Hall Of Rest, I had my sweatshirt laid over her body, for it to be cremated with her. It had been embroidered with "Amanda and Tia" and I knew I would never wear it again.

We were told it would take two hours, so we had a wander around the Crematorium gardens, then drove to a nearby village to pass some time.

We returned half an hour early. As we entered the waiting room, the lady said that, at the same moment I walked in, Tia's ashes had come through ready to be picked up. She said it happens sometimes. I felt warmed by it. It was like Tia knew I had come to take her home.

The next day, I went berserk with the Hoover, cleaning the house from top to bottom, every nook and cranny. I had to keep busy.

I was running the nozzle of the Hoover along the skirting board and I stopped and stood a while for a breather. I thought to myself, that I wished I had kept a chunk of her fur. I had been asked at the Crematorium if I wanted to do this but had turned it down. I didn't want to hack into her beautiful coat. I looked down to where I had just sucked up every last particle of dust and there, on top of the carpet, was a small group of her hairs, as though they had just been put there. I stared at them and thought how very strange, the carpet was absolutely spotless a second ago and I Hoovered them up without thinking.

Just after her death, the visits and strange happenings were more frequent. The first time that I saw her was three weeks after her death. I was walking through the telly room to go upstairs. I saw her whole body lying how she often used to, with her back against the sofa, her head up, ears casually erect, and watching the telly, that was on, the way she so often used to.

Tia loved the telly. She used to ask for it to be turned on, by staring at it with her nose close to the screen, yapping at it and wagging her stump of a tail (I had taught her to ask for what she wanted). I always turned it on for her but like a mother with a child, I had to monitor what she watched, because if there were any guns, or a baddy was creeping up on a goodie, she'd be up and barking at the screen and trying to bite the offending person, or the gun. She also used to listen to the music. When it changed to suspense, she was instantly there, ready for what was about to happen. To try to put a stop to this, I used to hit the "mute" button. This would work for about two days, until Tia's intelligence overrode it. She would watch the body language of the actors, or the guns being pointed.

Shortly after her death, I had my brother's two dogs come to stay while he was away on holiday. I let them use Tia's bed, the one she was euthanased on, which was a thick grey Vetbed type.

After they had left, I washed the bed, took it upstairs, and dumped it in a heap on the bedroom floor. The next morning, right on the top was a little white feather.

I found this comforting and started to collect white feathers from around the house, in unusual places.

About one week after 'seeing' Tia watching the telly, I was walking around Thame Agricultural Show. In the past, I always used to take Tia everywhere with me, until age started creeping up on her and it got too much for her.

I was walking just ahead of my partner, Nick, looking at the stalls, when out of the corner of my left eye, I saw what was like looking down on top of a dog's back, by the side of my leg. It was a black mass, moving along on my left side, where Tia always walked. It lasted a few seconds, and then it was gone. No-one was near me, only green grass around me, so it could not have been anyone's bag, or anything like that. I felt Tia was walking with me.

This was the first of two partial sightings.

My bedroom has a little window opposite the main window. The little window has no curtain, so at night, even with the lights off, you can still make out things in the room, especially with our next-door neighbours' outside light on.

One night, I was lying on my bed with my back to the little window. I heard a noise in the room, and rolled over to check what it was. Tia was in the middle of the room, and walked up to my face as I lay in bed.

I looked away from her to turn on the bedside light, so I could see her more clearly. When I looked back, she was gone. I desperately wished I hadn't turned away to put the light on, but felt hugely comforted to have seen her, and that she was letting me know she was still with me.

One afternoon / early evening, I was standing near the front door, talking to Nick, who was leaning on the corner of the dining room table bench, when behind him I saw a black mass; Tia's height. It moved from Tia's water bowl, (which has never been moved and stays down for visiting dogs; as does her bed), across the room, before it disappeared. It was as though Tia had had a drink and was casually walking back through the room, the same as she used to. Nick did not see this as he had his back to it.

But, what he did witness one day – and I'm so glad he did or I don't think anybody would have believed me, – was Tia's collar leaving the end of the curtain rail and landing between my feet!

After Tia died, I hung her collars, (the one she always wore and her special Swarovski diamante one), on the end of the curtain rail near the door.

One day, as I came in from the door, just as I walked past the window where the collars hang, her diamante collar landed between my feet and stopped me in my tracks. Instantly in my head, came, "I'm still with you".

I looked at Nick and said, "How did that happen?" He said he didn't know. I picked up the collar and hung it back on the curtain rail, then very quickly tried opening and shutting the door, trying to create as much of a draught as possible to see if that could have been the reason but it didn't budge. The collars have hung there for nearly two years and this was the only time it happened.

Nick tried the same thing, to see if a draught could have caused it but he had no success either.

And speaking of draughts, I still have my "Sympathy" cards for Tia on the mantelpiece above the fireplace. At the moment, I can't bring myself to take these down. Twice, when I have been walking past, one of the cards has just 'fallen' forward and gently rested on my shoulder. No draught.

The same sort of thing happened when Nick and I were away in Scotland. I had taken Tia's picture with me and put it on the mantelpiece. On one occasion, as I walked past, it just 'fell' forward and rested on my shoulder; like the sympathy cards. It was the only time it did it. Again, I tried creating a draught and I could just get it to fall by going frantic, waving the door back and forth but no such draught, or anything like it, was created when I ambled past. *

*****

Earlier this year, (2006), was the first time I smelt her in the house. It was very upsetting but a wonderful thing to have experienced. To feel her so close to me after death, through her visits, I feel she is letting me know she is still with me.

Tia's favourite spot to lie was at the bottom of the stairs, which come straight down into the sitting room. I used to step over her at the bottom when I came down the stairs.

After she died, I found I was purposely stepping over her 'space' at the bottom of the stairs. It was weird but I felt I had to put my foot 'over her' at the base of the stairs, or I would be stepping on top of her. I was annoyed at Nick for stepping on 'her spot', though I never told him because it sounded daft! To this day, I mostly miss her spot when I come down the stairs.

Anyway, earlier this year, in a hurry one day getting ready to go to the doctor's, I was stepping over 'her spot' coming down the stairs, when I smelt her. It stopped me dead in my tracks. I could not believe what I had just smelt. I was riveted to the spot. I moved my head very slightly from side to side a fraction at a time, trying to find her smell again but it was gone. The only way I can describe it, is that it was as though her smell had been 'bottled' and someone had run it past, close under my nose.

I tried moving, very slowly, just a footstep either way, still sniffing the air but she was gone.

I walked a couple of steps away and sat on the sofa, in shock and disbelief as to what had just happened. I had been sitting for only a few moments when it happened again. It was just like her smell was run under my nose again.

Again, I was sniffing the air, moving my head a fraction at a time, trying to find that particular spot where I had smelt her. I sat for a little while on the sofa, not really wanting to move, in case her smell came back but I had to get ready for the doctor's appointment. I got up and walked into the kitchen, thinking about what had just happened. As I entered the kitchen, her aroma hit me again and again it stopped me dead in my tracks and had me sniffing the air. I went and sat on the sofa and cried my eyes out, reflecting on what had just happened.

With each 'happening', I feel she is letting me know she is still with me.

Our bond in life was so incredibly strong and unusually close.

My partner, Nick, told me he always knew when I was on my way home, because approximately ten minutes before I'd arrive home, Tia would get up from where she was lying, walk to the front door, then lay down and wait, ready to greet me when I walked in. He said Tia only went to lie down by the door when I would have been just a few miles away and that she never got it wrong - I always drove up a few minutes later. This would happen at any time of the day. I had always assumed she just liked lying there, until Nick told me the real reason.

My last visit to date was May 2006. I was awoken in my bed early in the morning by the very strong smell of wet dog. Not "stinky" smelly, Tia never smelt like that, just 'wet dog'. I cleared the duvet from my face, so I could concentrate on the smell and take it in. I could hear the rain on the bedroom window; it was raining quite hard outside. I just thought "Tia" and relaxed, whilst lying on my back, taking in her smell and trying to savour the moment. It only lasted approximately 15 seconds, then it was gone and my room seemed so empty, with only the sound of the rain hammering down outside. This was the second time I smelt her.

Every visit I get, I wonder if it will be my last. I dearly hope not. I have a Cherished Number Plate, TIA 96, which, at the moment, - short-term, is on my seventeen-year-old VW Polo. The number plate is worth considerably more than the car

Every time I look at my TIA 96 number plate, I quietly do so with pride, as memories gently tug at my heart-strings. I think what a special gift it was and privilege, to have owned such a wonderful and talented dog. I feel truly blessed. We had twelve wonderful years together and I still think about her daily and miss her dreadfully. Like the Rainbow Guide's prayer that I mentioned earlier, I too "Thank you God, for Tia" ...a dog in a lifetime.

*I received the following e-mail from Amanda on 14.7.06 -*

Dear Wendy

Just something that might be of interest to you. Nick and I can't figure it out, my mobile phone is one that takes photos. When we were up in Scotland I took a photo of Tia's picture that is in black and white, (the one that fell on my shoulder), to show up on the front of my phone and to show a larger picture of Tia on the inside when I open it up.

What is so unusual is the little picture on the front of the phone is black and white just like the original, but the larger picture on the inside of the phone is in colour!

When I first told Nick about it he 'poo pooed' it, He said it wasn't what I thought it was, and was probably the lighting I took the picture in, or the camera in the phone. But I had one black and white picture, and one colour picture both from the same black and white photo; it didn't add up. The colour picture has the right shades of black and tan on Tia's face. It's not just a colour cast over the picture, as the pale back- ground hasn't gone brown at all.

What I did a couple of day's ago, it never  entered my head to do it before, was to take a photo of the same picture of Tia, but with Nick's phone (which is exactly the same make and model as mine).

The result was quite astonishing. Nick's phone showed a black and white picture on the front, and showed a black and white picture on the inside, as it is meant to do.

If you are ever down this way and would like to see this please let us know.

Best wishes
Amanda

P.S. I am now terrified of losing my phone!

*****

*(See photos page 78 & 79)*

* *This particular part of Amanda's story reminds me of something that happened on several occasions, for quite a while after we lost Sweep.  When I was either near, or walking through, the office, the old computer printer we had, would suddenly spring into life and spit out a piece of A4 paper, always with a tiny red heart printed in the top right-hand corner.  With love from Sweep?*

*The all-singing/all-dancing printer we have now has never done it.*

# Pat & Isobel

***Pat's Irish Wolfhound Isobel was a half-sister to Sweep, both having the same father, Toby, who also belonged to Pat and husband Peter.***

Isobel was four years old when she died of bloat in April 2005, following two operations to try to save her life. This was a double blow for Pat, as she had previously lost Isobel's mother, at just five years of age.

Isobel's body was cremated and her ashes were returned to Pat in a casket, which she put on the hearth in the empty fireplace in the living-room; as a 'temporary' resting-place, until she and husband Peter could decide where it was to 'live' permanently.

Towards the end of July, a friend of Pat's arrived to stay, bringing her dogs along with her as they were all going to a show a few days later.

Pat and her friend decided to go shopping and as her friend's dogs were in the kennel that normally belonged to Liam, (another of Pat's Wolfhounds), Liam had to stay in the kitchen, while Cillian Wolfhound, who normally lived in the kitchen, was put in the living-room, which was where Isobel always used to live before she passed over and where her ashes now lay in their casket.

*(This 'who can we put where' scenario probably sounds familiar to anyone who has several dogs!)*

The shopping trip duly over, Pat and friend returned home.

Normally, Pat would have expected the dogs to 'go demented' on her return, barking, howling and jumping up and down at the patio doors that lead from the kitchen onto the concrete yard at the side of the house.

Instead, it was quiet, with Liam just standing by the patio door and no sign of Cillian at all. There is a stable-door between the kitchen and the living-room and Pat would have expected, at the very least, that Cillian would have his head over the bottom half of the door, if not his front paws as well.

When she looked over the door to see where Cillian was, he was lying, (upright on his haunches), on the living room floor, in exactly the place that Isobel used to lie. Beside his paws and at least six feet away from the hearth, was the casket containing Isobel's ashes.

Pat couldn't believe what she was seeing and thought he must have somehow picked up the casket in his mouth, or pushed it with his nose or paw, to move it so far from the hearth but when she examined the casket she could find no marks of any kind on it; no teeth marks, no slobber, no scratches, nothing to indicate that Cillian had any part in moving it. To this day she still cannot explain how it got there, or why the dogs were so quiet when she returned home.

*****

*Steve and I visited Pat and Peter on Sunday 9th. October '05 and during dinner, Pat told us about Isobel's casket moving, which quite amazed us, because up to this point we thought that both Pat and Peter regarded this sort of thing with more than a little scepticism! Steve then told her that, as we had walked through to the dining-room, just as he passed through the door from the kitchen, he had 'seen' a dog run past him. He said it had a problem with a front teat and that an old lady had 'told' him he should point that out to Pat, so that she would recognise the dog. She did – eventually. She remembered that 'Abby', a bitch from the first litter she ever bred, had had that problem. We wondered if the old lady might be Ruth Jenkins, a long standing President of the Irish Wolfhound Club, who died in 2004. She was a good friend of Pat and Peter's and would have known Abby well.*

*(Between us, over the last two years, we have lost a good many hounds and I did remark to Pat on one occasion, previous to this visit, that I thought Ruth was collecting them all up!)*

*The day after our visit, Monday 10th October '05, Steve's alarm, which is never altered and is always set for 5.45am, went off at 6.25am instead. Later the same morning, the battery in the smoke alarm on the landing started to beep, to say the battery was low. Coincidence?*

*Our next visit to Pat and Peter was on Sunday 15th. January 2006, following a show. We live two hours travelling time apart and so, tend to time visits to coincide with shows in the area. We had just finished one of Pat's scrumptious pastas and Steve had gone out to the van to check the dogs. It was getting dark. When he came back indoors, he told Peter that there was a dog loose on the track. It had run past him and disappeared into the darkness at the end of the track, before the gate. Peter said there shouldn't be any dogs out but he went to check anyway. The gate at the end of the track prevents any loose dogs from leaving the property, so whoever was out couldn't escape but when Peter came back he said he couldn't find a dog, or see any sign of one. He checked all the kennels and everyone was where they should be and all the indoor dogs were present and accounted for.*

*Two days later, Toby died. Peter went out in the morning and found him dead in his kennel. As there were no signs of any distress, Peter assumes that he probably had a heart attack and died in his sleep. He was, of course, Isobel's father (and Sweep's). We all wonder if the dog that Steve saw was Isobel, waiting for her dad. The track was her favourite haunt (forgive the unintended pun!)*

*****

# Brenda and Tasha

### Brenda wrote -

A few months ago I lost my dear little Lhasa Apso, Tasha. She was nine years old and the puppy I kept from the one and only litter that I bred. She was my husband's treasure and he is devastated even now, ten months later. The funny thing is, that my 12 year old Shih Tzu, Molly, has taken over doing some of the things that Tasha alone used to do, for instance, she would run and scratch at the back door about six to eight times an evening, so that my husband would get up from his chair, then she would rush straight back into the lounge and find a ball, hoping that he would throw it for her to fetch. If that did not work enough times, she would sit at his feet with a toy in her mouth and look so forlorn. Molly never used to do these things. It is almost as though Tasha has asked her to play with Dad.

*****

# Gillian, Valerie and Clover

**Gillian and her sister Valerie have expanded their love of dogs into a dog and model car museum called 'Cloverlands'. The following is taken from Valerie's letter –**

Clover was born on Valentine's Day 1974. She was the runt of a litter of fourteen and so tiny she could fit into your hand. She came to us at just a few hours old and we hand-reared her and seven of her siblings. I took on the care of Clover, (so called because of a white mark on her head, like a four leaved clover), while Gillian cared for the stronger pups. I would get up three or four times a night to feed her. Mum called her 'the knob' because she was so small and she and I became known as 'the inseparables'. I would leave her in mum's care, on a bed of cotton wool on the storage heater in the kitchen, while I went to work and my first question on returning home was always, 'How is the knob?'

She survived against all odds and grew into the most delightful little dog, loved by all who met her. As she grew, it became apparent that she was mostly Whippet and she was so gentle that all living things loved and trusted her, so much so, that on one occasion, she even let a pet monkey sit on her back.

She also loved riding in cars. Our Hillman Minx had gone for repair and although we didn't know when it would be returned, the garage had said they would drive it back when it was ready. Mum and I were in the kitchen when Clover suddenly began to get very excited, running up to the door and wagging her tail. I said to mum 'I think Minxie (the car) must be on the way back, just look at Clover'. Sure enough, about ten minutes later, Minxie arrived and as soon as the door was opened, Clover ran straight out, jumped into the car and settled on the parcel shelf. She had been right but the car must have been five miles or more away when she started to get excited.

\*\*\*\*\*

Sadly, Clover died when she was just six years old, from what we now think was an auto-immune related disease. To me it was like losing a child.

Not long after, I was walking home from work, along a busy road, from which the lane to our house led off. I was waiting to cross over, when I became aware of a little brown dog, just like Clover, running along the pavement on the same side as me. To my horror, she decided to cross the road with the cars still coming. She ran between them but they apparently didn't see her, as they did not slow down or sound their horns. I turned away and waited, with a sick heart, for the awful bump but it didn't come. Instead, I saw the dog turn down our drive. When at last I could safely cross, I looked for the dog but there was no sign of her.

I felt Clover had come back to tell me she would always be there for me.

We still have 'Clovette', the little car built in her memory and our museums are named after her.

*****

# The Power Of The Dog

There is sorrow enough in the natural way
From men and women to fill our day;
And when we are certain of sorrow in store,
Why do we always arrange for more?
*Brothers and sisters, I bid you beware
Of giving your heart to a dog to tear.*

Buy a pup and your money will buy
Love unflinching that cannot lie – –
Perfect passion and worship fed
By a kick in the ribs or a pat on the head.
*Nevertheless it is hardly fair
To risk your heart for a dog to tear.*

When the fourteen years which Nature permits
Are closing in asthma, or tumour, or fits,
And the vet's unspoken prescription runs
To lethal chambers or loaded guns,
*Then you will find – – it's your own affair – –
But … you've given your heart to a dog to tear.*

When the body that lived at your single will,
With its whimper of welcome, is stilled (how still!)
When the spirit that answered your every mood
Is gone – –wherever it goes – –for good,
*You will discover how much you care,
And will give your heart to a dog to tear.*

We've sorrow enough in the natural way,
When it comes to burying Christian clay.
Our loves are not given, but only lent,
At compound interest of cent per cent.
Though it is not always the case, I believe,
That the longer we've kept 'em, the more do we grieve;

For, when debts are payable, right or wrong,
A short-time loan is as bad as a long – –
*So why in – –Heaven (before we are there)*
*Should we give our hearts to a dog to tear?*

**Rudyard Kipling**

*(ANSWERS ON A POSTCARD PLEASE! -   W.M. Tugby)*

# Lord Hugh Dowding

Air Chief Marshal, Lord Hugh Dowding, was born in Moffat, Scotland in 1882 and died, aged 87 years, in 1970. He was educated at Winchester College and went on to the Royal Military Academy, Woolwich. He was Commander-In-Chief of RAF Fighter Command during the Battle of Britain and became Air Chief Marshall in 1937.

He was a great humanitarian, his pilots in Fighter Command being known as 'Dowding's Chicks' and he was also a devoted animal lover and welfarist.

Following his retirement, he became interested in Spiritualism, believed in reincarnation and gave many public talks on the subjects. His first book 'Many Mansions' was published in 1943 and his second 'Lychgate', in 1945. In the latter, he describes his meetings, (in sleep-state), with dead RAF boys and how they continued to fly fighter planes from mountain-tops, from 'runways of light'. Years after publication of this book, a former pilot in his command remarked that, 'at that stage we thought Stuffy *(Lord Dowding's nickname)* had gone a bit ga ga.'

In his second book, 'Lychgate', Lord Dowding describes, how his late wife Muriel; who died two years after they were married, and is known in the spirit world as Clarice; is speaking from the spirit world and helping him to understand about the future life of animals.

***The following extract is taken from 'Lychgate' -***
"Some people say there are no animals 'Far On'; I can't believe that. Surely even in the Highest Heaven a bird must sing or a dog bark. They are part of the Creator, just as we are. It can't be just my love. Surely they must be there."

(Oughtn't they themselves to be progressing?)

"How do we know that there aren't higher forms of animal life? What about flowers? Aren't *they* part of God too? I will find out. I can travel quite a long way *inward* now, and I'll go as far as I can and find out where they leave off."

About a fortnight later we received the following:

*Clarice.* "There are animals everywhere – right into the celestial spheres, at least what are celestial to me. I have found them everywhere.

"There is one place which seems to belong to them alone. None of us lives there. I went with a friend to visit them. We had to cross a 'space'; it was like a void. It is so hard to find the correct word. That is the best I can do – a void. Then we were among them.

"It is a rather beautiful place in its way. Great crags and ravines and woods and rivers: I saw lions and leopards and many wild beasts. They were all quite 'tame' and did not seem to mind us. One beautiful cheetah even followed me round.

"The birds are so lovely I find it difficult to describe them and their song so clear and exquisite; it is sheer joy to listen.

"Beautiful trees and flowers are everywhere, and butterflies and all winged creatures.

"My friend showed me a valley where there were some strange animals, some so beautiful in form and so graceful in movement one felt spellbound. These are some of the earth's future inhabitants, I was told.

"Domestic animals were there too, dogs and cats and horses. All happy together, but any animal which is greatly loved by one of us seems to be much finer in every way than his fellows. I mean that he looks finer too – more graceful, shinier coat, more alert.

"Pets (which can only become pets by mutual love and consent) can live with us. I have my two dogs and a cat and three horses near to me. I seem to collect them somehow.

"In my search for the animals I went as far as I could reach into the Light and I found them all the way. But only the pets. The farther they are from their own place, the more they depend on their Love Guardian.

"My friend told me that they only exist on the Inner Planes because of the Love Bond.

"One great Shining One has a beautiful leopard as his companion. My friend told me the leopard had once saved His earth life, a long time ago, and the 'tamed animal' of those long-ago days has never been separated from the love of his Guardian.

"Another friend in the 5th Sphere from Earth has a gazelle as a pet, and another a beautiful Borzoi. Dogs are more plentiful, I find, than any other animal, lots and lots of small ones. There are a lot of cats too.

"One thing I noticed that the animals in the Inner Planes seem larger than their prototypes elsewhere. Pekingese for instance are quite large dogs. Love is the secret of their growth.

\*\*\*\*\*

*So, you see, this isn't a new concept at all and no-one could ever question Lord Dowding's credibility; even if back then they did think he might be a bit 'ga-ga'!*

# EXTRACT FROM 'MANY MANSIONS'

## By Lord Dowding

'Look forward to Death as something to be infinitely welcomed when your life's work is done.  Do not mourn or pity those who have gone before you but think of them as fortunate.  If you loved them here, continue to love them in your heart until you meet them again.'

# *In Conclusion*

Well, sadly, that's all for this book but what an incredible journey of discovery it has been and how privileged I feel, to have been entrusted with the task of sharing these stories with you.

I personally have gained so much from all of this, both spiritually and emotionally but also in the many friendships I've made along the way.

One matter that has troubled me though, concerns the letters and phone calls I've had from time to time, asking for help and advice after the death or disappearance of a much-loved pet. I hope I've listened sympathetically and that any advice I've given has been a help but I'm not an expert in these matters and sometimes I have to admit, I've felt totally inadequate to deal with the problem I've been confronted with. To that end, I felt it might be appropriate to include the contact details of a pet bereavement counselling service, which has people trained in this kind of work, who will listen and more importantly, be able to advise.

That doesn't mean that you can't phone me, just that I may not be the best person to help you, though of course, I'm always willing to listen and I'm still collecting ADC stories – who knows, there may yet be a third Rainbow Bridge book!

If you have a story you would like to share, you can either write to me at :-

Penlleinau, Blaencaron, Tregaron, Ceredigion, Wales SY25 6HL.

Or - Telephone/Fax (01974) 299000

Or - E-mail: Rynchanon@nightwing.fsbusiness.co.uk

# PET BEREAVEMENT COUNSELLING

The Pet Bereavement Support Service (PBSS) is run by two charities, The Blue Cross and the Society for Companion Animal Studies (SCAS). It was launched in 1994. As well as offering help, support and counselling to bereaved owners, it offers training in pet bereavement support to veterinary staff and the general public. The training course is accredited by the Open College Network.

Telephone Befrienders complete a six-month supervised training course and receive calls in their own homes. They offer a 'listening ear' to bereaved owners, working through the loss of their pet/s.

The Support Line number is:- 0800 096 6606

The helpline is open 7 days a week 8.30am – 8.30pm with an answerphone outside these hours.

If you prefer to write about how you are feeling, (available to both children and adults), you can contact a trained Email Befriender via the E-mail Support Service which was launched in 2002.

To use this service, e-mail: pbssmail@bluecross.org.uk

******

PBSS is a member of the British Association for Counselling and Psychotherapy and the Telephone Helplines Association.

******

# *Bibliography*

BUTALA  Sharon - 'Wild Stone Heart', An Apprentice In The Fields
Published by Virago Press 2001.

DOWDING  Lord  -  'Many Mansions'
Published by Rider and Company, London
(Random House Group Ltd.)  1943.

DOWDING  Lord, Air Chief Marshal - 'Lychgate'
Published by Rider and Company, London.
(Random House Group Ltd.) 1945.

GUGGENHEIM  Bill and Judy - 'Hello From Heaven'
Published by Bantam Books 1996

McCOURT  Frank. - 'Angela's Ashes' Published by Flamingo.
First published in GB by HarperCollins Publishers 1996

HADDON Celia - 'Faithful To The End "Daily Telegraph"
Anthology of Dogs'
Published by Headline Book Publishing Ltd. (1991)